## Early Praise for *Advanced Functional Programming with Elixir*

Joe has given Elixir developers the toolkit we didn't know we needed. This isn't abstract functional programming theory; it's the practical foundation that transforms how you solve complex problems and how your team thinks about solutions together. Read this book, then share it with your team. You'll wonder how you built systems without it.

➤ **Nicholas Henry**
  Software Developer

The Effect monad chapter alone is worth the price. Instead of Tasks firing off immediately, you can build them up, compose them, and run them when you're ready. This isn't theory—it's practical FP that solves real Elixir problems.

➤ **Jacob Luetzow**
  Elixir Mentor

An excellent, well-written, and engaging book. Even as someone experienced with functional programming, I gained a deeper understanding of familiar concepts. The balance of theory and practice is spot-on, with a seamless flow from chapter to chapter. Best of all, the lessons extend beyond Elixir to any language that embraces functional programming principles.

➤ **Fred Daoud**
  Pragmatic Bookshelf Author

This book offers a glimpse into many concepts from academia and other functional programming languages that were completely new to me. I look forward to using the concepts from this book to write better, more maintainable code.

➤ **Nicholas Moen**
  Software Developer

# Advanced Functional Programming with Elixir

Model Behavior, Manage Complexity,
and Maximize Maintainability

Joseph Koski

The Pragmatic Bookshelf

Dallas, Texas

# Pragmatic Bookshelf

See our complete catalog of hands-on, practical,
and Pragmatic content for software developers:
*https://pragprog.com*

Sales, volume licensing, and support:
*support@pragprog.com*

Derivative works, AI training and testing,
international translations, and other rights:
*rights@pragprog.com*

The team that produced this book includes:

| | |
|---|---|
| Publisher: | Dave Thomas |
| COO: | Janet Furlow |
| Executive Editor: | Susannah Davidson |
| Series Editor: | Sophie DeBenedetto |
| Development Editor: | Adaobi Obi Tulton |
| Copy Editor: | L. Sakhi MacMillan |

ISBN-13: 979-8-88865-179-7
Book version: P1.0—November, 2025

# Contents

Acknowledgments . . . . . . . . . . . ix

Introduction . . . . . . . . . . . . xi

1. **Build FunPark: Model Real-World Data** . . . . . . 1
   Define the Ride Model                                    2
   Implement FastPasses for Priority Access                 4
   Model the Patrons                                        5
   Speak the Language                                       7
   What You've Learned                                      7

2. **Implement Domain-Specific Equality with Protocols** . . . 9
   Polymorphic Equality                                    10
   Implement Equality for FunPark Contexts                 11
   Equality Is Contextual                                  17
   Transform Inputs Before Matching                        17
   Harness Equality for Collections                        21
   What You've Learned                                     26

3. **Create Flexible Ordering with Protocols** . . . . . . 29
   Define Order with a Protocol                            30
   Implement Order for FunPark Contexts                    31
   Transform Inputs Before Comparison                      34
   Harness Order for Collections                           37
   Reverse the Order                                       41
   Reduce Repetitive Code with Macros                      42
   What You've Learned                                     44

4. **Combine with Monoids** . . . . . . . . . . 45
   Define the Protocol 46
   Combine Numbers with Sum 47
   Combine Equality 51
   Combine Order 56
   Generalize Maximum 61
   Manage Complexity 66
   What You've Learned 69

5. **Define Logic with Predicates** . . . . . . . . . 71
   Simple Predicates 72
   Combine Predicates 73
   Predicates That Span Contexts 76
   Compose Multi-Arity Functions with Curry 78
   Harness Predicates for Collections 81
   Model the FastPass 85
   Fold Conditional Logic 90
   What You've Learned 92

6. **Compose in Context with Monads** . . . . . . . 93
   Build the Monad 94
   Model Neutrality with Identity 98
   What You've Learned 105

7. **Access Shared Environment with Reader** . . . . . 107
   Build the Structures 108
   Monad Behaviors 108
   Avoid Prop Drilling 109
   Dependency Injection 110
   Shared Configuration 111
   What You've Learned 112

8. **Manage Absence with Maybe** . . . . . . . . 115
   Build the Structures 116
   Fold Branches 117
   Lift Other Contexts 120
   Bridge Elixir Patterns 122

Define Equality 124
Establish Order 126
Lift Custom Comparisons 127
Model Absence in a Monoid 129
Implement the Monadic Behaviors 131
Refine Lists 136
Filter Within Composition 142
What You've Learned 146

9. **Model Outcomes with Either** . . . . . . . **149**
Structure of Either 150
Validation 151
From Bind to Combine 160
Make Errors Explicit 169
What You've Learned 177

10. **Coordinate Tasks with Effect** . . . . . . **179**
Build the Effect 180
Deferred Transformation 184
Effectful Store 187
Maintenance Repository 189
Inject Behavior, Not Configuration 197
Flip the Logic 201
What You've Learned 208

11. **Answers** . . . . . . . . . . . **209**
Equality Chapter Answers 209
Order Chapter Answers 210
Monoid Chapter Answers 212
Predicate Chapter Answers 213
Maybe Chapter Answers 214
Either Chapter Answers 216

**Bibliography** . . . . . . . . . . **219**

# Acknowledgments

This book wouldn't exist without the generosity of my reviewers. They caught mistakes, challenged assumptions, and pushed me to sharpen every idea until it stood on its own.

I'm especially grateful to Uberto Barbini, Fred Daoud, Robert Engler, Bryan Green, Chris Kincanon, Nic Moen, Steven Schultz, Stefan Turalski, and Michael Xavier for their careful reading and thoughtful feedback.

Thanks to Dave Thomas and his Pragmatic Bookshelf team, not only for publishing this book but also for the years of care, craft, and influence they've brought to technical publishing. Their work has shaped how we learn, teach, and grow as developers.

I also thank Sophie DeBenedetto, series editor, and Adaobi Obi Tulton, development editor, whose insight and guidance helped shape the book from first draft to final form.

The Elixir community has been a constant source of inspiration. The libraries, talks, and conversations that flow through it made this project possible and reminded me that programming is at its best when it's shared.

# Introduction

The question I hear most often about functional programming is "Why bother?" It feels like overkill. Code reuse is a myth, and most abstractions rot faster than they're shared. Instead of clarity, you get a maze of indirection. Onboarding suffers. And in the end, the business just wants working code—they don't care how you get there.

Fair enough. Functional programming won't fix a broken project any more than switching frameworks will fix a broken team. If your domain is unclear, your boundaries are a mess, and no one understands how the parts fit together, adding monads won't help. At best, you'll just find new ways to express confusion.

But if you care about the long game, about building systems that are easier to understand and safer to change, then functional programming helps—not because it's clever but because it demands clarity. The goal is confidence: confidence that your code behaves, that your logic composes, that your abstractions scale.

Because once fear sets in, no one wants to touch the core—they just patch the edges and hope nothing breaks.

I, like many developers, come from a music background. There, mastery was unmistakable—you could hear it. From the outside, it looked like talent. But inside, we knew better: it came from hours of focused practice—not playing what you already knew, but slogging through the uncomfortable bits just beyond your reach. As Anders Ericsson explains in *Peak [EP16]*, the mythic 10,000-hour rule is nonsense. It's not the time, it's the grind.

But why grind at all? As Daniel Pink shows in *Drive [Pin09]*, we're motivated by mastery. We want to understand, improve, and take control. Functional programming helps by sharpening how we think—its mental models are explicit and composable. They shift our focus from sequences to transformations, from behavior to relationships.

Most functional programming books drop you into the deep end—dense syntax, abstract theory, and jargon with little connection to real code. This one takes a different path. It doesn't pretend learning functional programming is easy. It's not. But mastery depends on knowing where you're going, step by step, with each concept building on the last—not by simplifying the ideas but by making them learnable: deliberate, cumulative, and within reach.

## How This Book Works

You'll start with foundational patterns like equality and ordering and build toward more powerful structures: monoids, predicates, and eventually monads. Each chapter adds a concept, connects it to what came before, and pushes a little further.

The examples are written for clarity, not production. They're minimal and focused—meant to show the shape of a problem rather than cover every edge case. Alongside the book, you'll find a production-ready library that implements these abstractions—fully tested, well documented, and ready to use.[1] It's also a good place to find minimal examples and quick references.

The goal of functional programming is to build systems that stay flexible as they grow—able to absorb new requirements without buckling. After all, the only measure of quality that matters is how well your code holds up under change.

## Who This Book Is For

This book is for developers who want to sharpen how they think about code. You might already be working in Elixir, or you might come from another language and are curious about functional programming or even about Elixir itself. No prior functional programming experience is required, just the ability to write basic programs in any modern language along with curiosity, patience, and a willingness to explore new ideas.

## Online Resources

- Visit the book's page on the Pragmatic Bookshelf website to download the code and access related resources.[2] If you own the ebook, each code example also includes a small gray box you can click to download the code snippet.

---

1.  https://hexdocs.pm/funx/readme.html
2.  https://pragprog.com/titles/jkelixir

- Alternatively, open the interactive Livebooks to run, edit, and experiment with the examples in your browser.[3]

- Join the conversation on the book's DevTalk forum to discuss topics, share ideas, and report errata that could shape future editions.[4]

- Bridge the gap between reading and doing with the Tutor, which gives your LLM the ability to leverage the Funx library to provide answers and feedback as you explore.[5]

- And remember to explore Funx, the production-ready library that implements these abstractions.[6]

## Conventions Used in This Book

This book builds functional programming mental models through the story of FunPark. We start with general FP patterns, apply them in the FunPark source code, and see these patterns in action through interactive sessions (iex). These interactive sessions appear shaded and are woven into the narrative.

The "Joe asks" asides answer the "what about …?" moments, and tip asides offer pointers to help the reader spot something important, clear up a misunderstanding, or make a connection.

With the map in hand, let's explore what's around the bend!

---

3.  https://www.funxlib.com/book-livebooks.html
4.  http://devtalk.com/books/advanced-functional-programming-with-elixir
5.  https://www.funxlib.com/tutor.html
6.  https://www.funxlib.com

# CHAPTER 1

# Build FunPark: Model Real-World Data

A theme park is more than just rides and attractions—it's a living system, constantly adjusting to keep guests moving while making their experience feel seamless and exciting. At any moment, visitors are making choices: rushing to the newest roller coaster, securing a FastPass, or deciding whether a classic ride is worth the wait. Meanwhile, behind the scenes, the park is in motion—managing crowds, adjusting wait times, prioritizing guests, and ensuring everything runs smoothly and safely.

We've been asked to build the system that runs FunPark. At first, it seems straightforward—track rides, guests, and wait times—but we quickly realize there's a lot we don't know. The business team doesn't have every answer, and even the experts are still figuring things out. Rather than trying to define everything up front, we'll take an iterative approach: building small, independent parts and refining them as we learn.

So where do we start?

Functional programming helps us manage this complexity by breaking problems into small, composable functions. These functions make behavior easier to reason about, test, and reuse—ideal for systems that grow and change over time. But structure matters too: without clear boundaries, even composable code becomes tangled.

To keep things organized, we'll apply the principles of *Domain-Driven Design [Eva03]*, dividing the system into *bounded contexts*. Each context owns part of the domain and defines how its data and behavior fit together. This lets us apply functional techniques within well-defined boundaries, ensuring that change stays local and models stay aligned with real-world concerns.

After some initial investigation, we discover that FunPark has three distinct areas: Rides, Patrons, and FastPass. We'll begin by meeting with domain experts to understand each context, starting with the Ride.

## Define the Ride Model

After discussions with our Ride expert, we identify the core attributes: a unique ID, a name, and parameters for minimum height and age requirements. We also learn that rides can go offline and include tags that describe their experience, such as :dark, :thrill, or :water.

```
lib/fun_park/ride.ex
defstruct id: nil,
          name: "Unknown Ride",
          min_age: 0,
          min_height: 0,
          wait_time: 0,
          online: true,
          tags: []

def make(name, opts \\ []) when is_binary(name) do
  %__MODULE__{
    id: :erlang.unique_integer([:positive]),
    name: name,
    min_age: Keyword.get(opts, :min_age, 0),
    min_height: Keyword.get(opts, :min_height, 0),
    wait_time: Keyword.get(opts, :wait_time, 0),
    online: Keyword.get(opts, :online, true),
    tags: Keyword.get(opts, :tags, [])
  }
end
```

In domain-driven design, a factory creates domain objects in a consistent way, keeping their internal structure loosely coupled from the rest of the system. The FunPark.Ride module follows this pattern by exposing a make/2 factory function for creating new rides.

The struct defines default values for each field. The make/2 function takes a name and an optional map of overrides. Fields not provided in the map fall back to defaults. Each ride is also assigned a unique ID using Erlang's :erlang.unique_integer/1.

## Run It

Before diving in, go to the book's website and download the finished project so you can run everything against the complete codebase.[1] The code snippets highlight key ideas, not every detail, and trying to piece them together into a working project will be frustrating. Also, seeing the full module in context often makes things clearer since it's easier to understand the structure as a whole.

If you prefer a more interactive experience, you can use the Livebooks.[2]

If you're starting from scratch and want to run the full project locally, check out *Installing Elixir*.[3]

Throughout this book, we'll use Elixir's interactive shell, iex, launched with the -S mix flag to compile the project and load its modules. To begin, open a terminal, navigate to the project directory, and run:

```
iex -S mix
```

Let's start with a task we'll be doing repeatedly throughout this book: generating a Ride.

```
iex> FunPark.Ride.make("Tea Cup", wait_time: 10, tags: [:family_friendly])
%FunPark.Ride{
  id: 3619,
  name: "Tea Cup",
  min_age: 0,
  min_height: 0,
  wait_time: 10,
  online: true,
  tags: [:family_friendly]
}
```

After the iex> prompt, we call make from the FunPark.Ride module to create a new ride. Here, we define a ride named Tea Cup with a wait time of 10 minutes and a :family_friendly tag. After pressing enter, the interactive shell evaluates the expression and prints the resulting FunPark.Ride struct, which includes our provided values along with logical defaults, such as no minimum age or height and an automatically assigned unique ID.

---

1. https://pragprog.com/titles/jkelixir
2. https://www.funxlib.com/book-livebooks.html
3. https://elixir-lang.org/install.html

Let's also create the Dark Mansion ride:

```
iex> dark_mansion = FunPark.Ride.make(
    "Dark Mansion",
    min_age: 14,
    tags: [:dark]
)
%FunPark.Ride{
  id: 3683,
  name: "Dark Mansion",
  min_age: 14,
  min_height: 0,
  wait_time: 0,
  online: true,
  tags: [:dark]
}
```

Again, we've set the required name and a few optional values, with the rest falling back to sensible defaults, giving us a consistent way to create rides.

Try creating a few rides of your own to get a feel for how it works.

## Implement FastPasses for Priority Access

The FunPark includes the FastPass, a system that helps manage demand for popular rides. After speaking with the FastPass experts, we learn that passes are tied to a specific ride and time.

With this, we can take a first crack at modeling FastPass:

```
lib/fun_park/fast_pass.ex
defstruct id: nil,
          ride: nil,
          time: nil

def make(%Ride{} = ride, %DateTime{} = time) do
  %__MODULE__{
    id: :erlang.unique_integer([:positive]),
    ride: ride,
    time: time
  }
end
```

Again, we use make/2 to control instance creation. Unlike Ride, FastPass has no optional elements, both the Ride and DateTime structs are required. Each FastPass also includes a system-wide unique ID, allowing us to differentiate passes for the same ride and time.

### Run It

Let's test our logic with the interactive shell running the mix script. First, create a time:

```
iex> datetime = DateTime.new!(~D[2025-06-01], ~T[13:00:00])
~U[2025-06-01 13:00:00Z]
```

Next, create a FastPass for dark_mansion with that time:

```
iex> fast_pass = FunPark.FastPass.make(dark_mansion, datetime)
%FunPark.FastPass{
  id: 3586,
  ride: %FunPark.Ride{
    id: 3490,
    name: "Dark Mansion",
    min_age: 14,
    min_height: 0,
    wait_time: 0,
    online: true,
    tags: [:dark]
  },
  time: ~U[2025-06-01 13:00:00Z]
}
```

This gives us a foundation for modeling time-based access.

## Model the Patrons

Let's imagine that until now, the development team has been calling the people in FunPark "guests." But after sitting down with the experts, we learn they use the term "patron." To stay aligned, we rename our bounded context from Guest to Patron. In bounded contexts, naming matters—terms should match the language used by the people who work in and understand that part of the domain.

As our discussions continue, more details come to light. Each patron has a ticket, a unique ID, and personal attributes such as name, height, and age. Patrons collect FastPasses, and tickets are tiered to grant different levels of access. They earn reward points as they engage with the park, and they have likes and dislikes that influence their choices and experiences.

To capture this, we define a struct for patrons (shown on the next page):

```
lib/fun_park/patron.ex
defstruct id: nil,
          name: nil,
          age: 0,
          height: 0,
          ticket_tier: :basic,
          fast_passes: [],
          reward_points: 0,
          likes: [],
          dislikes: []

def make(name, age, height, opts \\ [])
    when is_bitstring(name) and
         is_integer(age) and
         is_integer(height) and
         age > 0 and
         height > 0 do
  %__MODULE__{
    id: :erlang.unique_integer([:positive]),
    name: name,
    age: age,
    height: height,
    ticket_tier: Keyword.get(opts, :ticket_tier, :basic),
    fast_passes: Keyword.get(opts, :fast_passes, []),
    reward_points: Keyword.get(opts, :reward_points, 0),
    likes: Keyword.get(opts, :likes, []),
    dislikes: Keyword.get(opts, :dislikes, [])
  }
end
```

This time, we use make/4, requiring every patron to have a name, age, and height, while allowing ticket tier, FastPasses, and reward points to be set with logical defaults or optional values.

## Run It

Let's start with a patron named Alice, who has a FastPass:

```
iex> FunPark.Patron.make("Alice", 15, 120, fast_passes: [fast_pass])
%FunPark.Patron{
  id: 3618,
  name: "Alice",
  age: 15,
  height: 120,
  ticket_tier: :basic,
  fast_passes: [
    %FunPark.FastPass{
      id: 3586,
      ride: %FunPark.Ride{
        id: 3490,
```

```
      name: "Dark Mansion",
      min_age: 14,
      min_height: 0,
      wait_time: 0,
      online: true,
      tags: [:dark]
    },
    time: ~U[2025-06-01 13:00:00Z]
  }
 ],
 reward_points: 0,
 likes: [],
 dislikes: []
}
```

By aligning our names with domain language and capturing key attributes up front, we create a model that reflects how the park understands its patrons.

Now that the basics are in place, try creating your own Ride, FastPass, and Patron instances. Vary the attributes, explore how defaults behave, and see how everything fits together by issuing passes for different rides and times.

## Speak the Language

Language matters when building a complex system. To avoid confusion, we develop a *ubiquitous language*: a concept from domain-driven design (DDD) that refers to a shared vocabulary used consistently by developers, designers, and domain experts within a bounded context.

When our experts informed us that a guest is actually called a "patron," we embraced the change, refactoring our code to reflect this updated understanding. Aligning our terminology avoids translation, ensuring a direct connection between how concepts are discussed and how they are implemented.

We take a lightweight, practical approach to DDD throughout the book—for a deeper dive, see *Domain-Driven Design [Eva03]* by Eric Evans or *Domain Modeling Made Functional [Wla18]* by Scott Wlaschin.

## What You've Learned

It's tempting to try to define systems up front, but that's not how complex software is built. Instead, embrace iteration. Work with domain experts to refine understanding and let the design emerge over time.

Complex software is never finished, so our goal is to build a system that's easy to change and adapt as we learn. Functional programming helps break logic into small, composable components, while domain-driven design separates responsibilities. Together, they help manage complexity while keeping the system flexible as it evolves.

With a foundation in place, let's now turn to the question of comparison. In the next chapter, we'll define context-aware equality, using Elixir's protocols to express when one Patron, Ride, or FastPass should be considered the same—or different—from another.

> The purpose of FunPark is to build a shared mental representation that we can revisit and extend as we work through the process of learning functional programming. The best way to learn is to create a new problem to solve, your own mental representation, using FunPark as a guide or a fallback.

# CHAPTER 2

# Implement Domain-Specific Equality with Protocols

A production-ready Eq is available in the Funx library.[1]

Is that the same car that was in my driveway this morning, or does it just look like my car? Identity asks whether it's the *same* thing, while equality considers whether two things share similar characteristics.

Equality depends on the domain. In insurance, cars are equal if they share the same actuarial risks; in repairs, if they have compatible parts; and in sales, if they have comparable market value. If we want to know whether it's the same car—even if it's been repainted or has different seats—we rely on something unique, like a VIN. In software, we apply equality to identifiers to establish identity.

We've all used equality to deduplicate a list or check membership. But once we internalize the mental model—understanding equality as a domain-defined rule that shapes behavior—we can solve more sophisticated problems like memoization, caching, replay protection, and Bloom filters.

This chapter introduces our first Elixir protocol, using it to define equality in a way that reflects domain intent. That allows us to centralize logic, reduce duplication, and support higher-level operations.

---

1.  https://hexdocs.pm/funx/Funx.Eq.html

Eq defines equality through three rules:

- *Reflexivity:* a = a.
- *Symmetry:* If a = b, then b = a.
- *Transitivity:* If a = b and b = c, then a = c.

In each of our FunPark contexts, we've included an id field to represent identity. For example, two Ride records refer to the same ride when they share the same id. Equality is always defined within a bounded context. No meaningful comparison exists between a Ride and a Patron.

Equality logic has a way of getting scattered across a codebase. We want to keep Eq close to the core, where it belongs: defined once, in terms the domain understands, and reused everywhere.

Later in the chapter, we'll see how to reuse existing equality logic with tools like contramap and how Eq enables generic collection functions, such as deduplication and set operations.

## Polymorphic Equality

Life gets easier when equality is *polymorphic*—able to adapt to the kind of input it compares. In functional programming, polymorphism means defining behavior abstractly, so it applies across many types. Elixir doesn't have a static type system, but it does have structs: maps tagged with a module name. That tag becomes the dispatch key for protocols, allowing polymorphic behavior through dynamic dispatch. With this mechanism, the Eq protocol acts as a shared interface, and each struct can define what equality means in its own context.

As *Programming Elixir [Tho18]* notes, Elixir protocols give us a disciplined way to implement polymorphism.

lib/fun_park/eq.ex
```
defprotocol FunPark.Eq do
  @fallback_to_any true

  def eq?(a, b)

  def not_eq?(a, b)
end
```

This protocol specifies that anything implementing Eq must define two functions: eq?/2, which checks whether two values are equal, and not_eq?/2, which determines when they are not. We include both because, in some cases, checking for inequality can be more efficient than checking for equality.

Protocols in Elixir are resolved at runtime, so there are no compile-time guarantees. If we attempt to compare two values that lack an Eq implementation, the call raises a runtime error.

Elixir's @fallback_to_any directive provides a safeguard. If a type doesn't explicitly implement Eq, Elixir falls back to a generic implementation for Any.

lib/fun_park/eq.ex
```
defimpl FunPark.Eq, for: Any do
  def eq?(a, b), do: a == b
  def not_eq?(a, b), do: a != b
end
```

With this default implementation, FunPark.Eq.eq?/2 delegates unknown values to Elixir's built-in equality operators.

### Run It

Start Elixir's iex shell and run the mix script to compile the code and load the project.

```
iex -S mix
```

Using Elixir's == operator, we see that 1 is equal to 1 but not equal to 2:

```
iex> 1 == 1
true
iex> 1 == 2
false
```

Our eq?/2 protocol produces the same results:

```
iex> FunPark.Eq.eq?(1, 1)
true
iex> FunPark.Eq.eq?(1, 2)
false
```

By defining a shared interface for equality, we gain the flexibility to compare values in a way that fits each domain type. With a default in place, we're now ready to define context-aware equality.

## Implement Equality for FunPark Contexts

FunPark is constantly evolving—rides update wait times, and patrons earn reward points. Before we define equality, we need a reliable way to update data. To support that, we'll add a change/2 function to the Patron module.

```
lib/fun_park/patron.ex
def change(%__MODULE__{} = patron, attrs) when is_map(attrs) do
  attrs = Map.delete(attrs, :id)

  struct(patron, attrs)
end
```

Elixir's struct/2 function updates an existing struct by merging it with a map of new values. Only keys that match the struct's defined fields are applied; any extras are ignored, preserving the shape of the struct.

change/2 takes a Patron and a map of updates, removes the :id key to prevent changing the entity's identity, and returns a new Patron with the remaining fields applied. Because it returns the same type it receives, change/2 is *closed*.

> **Joe asks:**
> ## What Is Closure?
>
> In set theory, a set is *closed under an operation* if applying that operation to elements of the set always produces another element of the same set.
>
> In functional programming, we use the term similarly: a function satisfies *closure* if it returns the same type it receives.
>
> When each step in a pipeline stays within the same type, it becomes easy to chain transformations without extra wrappers, branching, or conversion logic.

A production-level change/2 should protect boundaries—similar to how changesets do in Ecto, as described in *Programming Ecto [WM19]*.

## Run It

Create a patron named Alice:

```
iex> alice_a = FunPark.Patron.make("Alice", 15, 150)
%FunPark.Patron{
  id: 3522,
  name: "Alice",
  age: 15,
  height: 150,
  ticket_tier: :basic,
  fast_passes: [],
  reward_points: 0,
  likes: [],
  dislikes: []
}
```

Alice decides to update her ticket to :premium:

```
iex> alice_b = FunPark.Patron.change(alice_a, %{ticket_tier: :premium})
%FunPark.Patron{
  id: 3522,
  name: "Alice",
  age: 15,
  height: 150,
  ticket_tier: :premium,
  fast_passes: [],
  reward_points: 0,
  likes: [],
  dislikes: []
}
```

From Elixir's perspective, alice_a and alice_b are not an exact match, so they are not equal:

```
iex> alice_a == alice_b
false
```

However, within the Patron context, this is wrong. Upgrading Alice's ticket doesn't make her a different patron; it just reflects a change in her attributes.

To implement equality for the Patron context, we use the Eq protocol and pattern match on the Patron struct.

## Implement the Eq Protocol

Here we're implementing the FunPark.Eq protocol for the FunPark.Patron struct. Elixir will dispatch to this implementation whenever the first argument of eq?/2 or not_eq?/2 functions is a Patron.

```
lib/fun_park/patron.ex
defimpl FunPark.Eq, for: FunPark.Patron do
  alias FunPark.Eq
  alias FunPark.Patron
  def eq?(%Patron{id: v1}, %Patron{id: v2}), do: Eq.eq?(v1, v2)
  def not_eq?(%Patron{id: v1}, %Patron{id: v2}), do: Eq.not_eq?(v1, v2)
end
```

Each function extracts the id field from both Patron structs and compares them using the generic Eq protocol. Because we haven't defined a custom implementation for integers, these calls fall back to the Eq implementation for Any, which uses Elixir's built-in comparison.

Technically, pattern matching on the first argument here is redundant; Elixir dispatches to this implementation only when the first argument is a Patron.

> **Joe asks:**
> ## Wait, Can't You Just Derive not_eq?
>
> You can. Ideally, not_eq? would default to the negation of eq?, but Elixir protocols don't support optional functions, so both must be defined. But that's just the protocol; your implementation is free to derive one from the other.

## Run It

First, let's regenerate our Patron structs:

```
iex> alice_a = FunPark.Patron.make("Alice", 15, 150)
iex> alice_b = FunPark.Patron.change(alice_a, %{ticket_tier: :premium})
```

FunPark knows that although these are different records, they refer to the same Patron:

```
iex> FunPark.Eq.eq?(alice_a, alice_b)
true
```

For those used to scripting languages like JavaScript, this might seem surprising—how does Elixir know these values are patrons?

By implementing FunPark.Eq for the Patron struct, we have, in a sense, taught Elixir how to recognize and determine equality for a Patron.

Eq uses *projection*, where a value is transformed—typically by extracting a field—so equality can be defined based on that simpler representation. This idea, which we'll revisit later as contramap, allows us to reuse existing comparisons on more complex structures.

## Ride Eq

We add the same logic to the FunPark.Ride context:

```
lib/fun_park/ride.ex
def change(%__MODULE__{} = ride, attrs) when is_map(attrs) do
  attrs = Map.delete(attrs, :id)

  struct(ride, attrs)
end
```

And we implement the Eq protocol:

```
lib/fun_park/ride.ex
defimpl FunPark.Eq, for: FunPark.Ride do
  alias FunPark.Eq
  alias FunPark.Ride
  def eq?(%Ride{id: v1}, %Ride{id: v2}), do: Eq.eq?(v1, v2)
  def not_eq?(%Ride{id: v1}, %Ride{id: v2}), do: Eq.not_eq?(v1, v2)
end
```

## Run It

Let's generate a Ride:

```
iex> ride_a = FunPark.Ride.make("Dark Mansion", min_age: 14, tags: [:dark])
%FunPark.Ride{
  id: 2210,
  name: "Dark Mansion",
  min_age: 14,
  min_height: 0,
  wait_time: 0,
  online: true,
  tags: [:dark]
}
```

And we'll update the wait time to 20 minutes.

```
iex> ride_b = FunPark.Ride.change(ride_a, %{wait_time: 20})
%FunPark.Ride{
  id: 2210,
  name: "Dark Mansion",
  min_age: 14,
  min_height: 0,
  wait_time: 20,
  online: true,
  tags: [:dark]
}
```

Again, from Elixir's perspective, these are not equal:

```
iex> ride_a == ride_b
false
```

But from the Ride context, updating the wait time does not make them different rides, and our Eq protocol evaluates them as true:

```
iex> FunPark.Eq.eq?(ride_a, ride_b)
true
```

> **Joe asks:**
> ## Can't We Just Use the Same change/1 Function?
>
> It might be tempting to define a shared utility function for change/2, but doing so would blur boundaries and undermine the separation between contexts.
>
> If we want a common interface for the idea of *changeable*, a protocol is a better fit; it gives us polymorphic behavior without coupling contexts together.

## FastPass Eq

And finally, we use the same pattern to implement change/2 for the FunPark.FastPass module.

```
lib/fun_park/fast_pass.ex
def change(%__MODULE__{} = fast_pass, attrs) when is_map(attrs) do
  attrs = Map.delete(attrs, :id)

  struct(fast_pass, attrs)
end
```

We also implement the Eq protocol for FastPass, comparing instances by their id fields:

```
lib/fun_park/fast_pass.ex
defimpl FunPark.Eq, for: FunPark.FastPass do
  alias FunPark.Eq
  alias FunPark.FastPass
  def eq?(%FastPass{id: v1}, %FastPass{id: v2}), do: Eq.eq?(v1, v2)
  def not_eq?(%FastPass{id: v1}, %FastPass{id: v2}), do: Eq.not_eq?(v1, v2)
end
```

This follows the same delegation strategy used for Patron, falling back to the Eq implementation for Any when comparing IDs.

## Run It

Generate a FastPass:

```
iex> tea_cup = FunPark.Ride.make("Tea Cup")
iex> datetime = DateTime.new!(~D[2025-06-01], ~T[13:00:00])

iex> pass_a = FunPark.FastPass.make(tea_cup, datetime)
```

Now update the ride on that pass:

```
iex> haunted_mansion = FunPark.Ride.make("Haunted Mansion")
iex> pass_b = FunPark.FastPass.change(pass_a, %{ride: haunted_mansion})
```

Elixir sees the difference:

```
iex> pass_a == pass_b
false
```

But our Eq implementation focuses only on ID and treats them as equal:

```
iex> FunPark.Eq.eq?(pass_a, pass_b)
true
```

Now that our Eq protocol is aware of domain contexts, we have a foundation for consistent comparisons.

As often happens, after implementing the logic for FastPasses, our Patron expert points out a problem: a patron can't be in two places at once. From their perspective, two passes scheduled for the same time are effectively duplicates.

## Equality Is Contextual

No problem, we can just adjust the FastPass implementation to target the time rather than the ID.

```
defimpl FunPark.Eq, for: FunPark.FastPass do
  alias FunPark.Eq
  alias FunPark.FastPass
  def eq?(%FastPass{time: v1}, %FastPass{time: v2}), do: Eq.eq?(v1, v2)

  def not_eq?(%FastPass{time: v1}, %FastPass{time: v2}),
    do: Eq.not_eq?(v1, v2)
end
```

But wait—we don't want to replace the default Eq for FastPass. Instead, we need an alternative Eq that considers two FastPasses equal if they occur at the same time.

## Transform Inputs Before Matching

If you've worked with lists, you're likely familiar with map, an implementation of a *functor*, which applies a function to transform something while preserving its structure. For a list, this means transforming each item. Functional programming also includes the *contravariant functor*, which transforms the input before it's processed. This is useful for abstractions like Eq and Ord, where we often want to transform a value before it enters the comparison, such as extracting a specific field or normalizing the input to ignore differences like case or formatting.

We'll cover functors in more detail in Transform with a Functor, on page 94.

Unlike some other functional languages, Elixir doesn't have a built-in contramap function, so we need to implement it ourselves.

```
defmodule FunPark.Eq.Utils do
  alias FunPark.Eq

  def contramap(f) do
    %{
      eq?: fn a, b -> Eq.eq?(f.(a), f.(b)) end,
      not_eq?: fn a, b -> Eq.not_eq?(f.(a), f.(b)) end
    }
  end
end
```

The contramap/1 function is a *higher-order transformer*: it takes an existing comparator and adapts it to work on a different type by applying a function *before* comparing values.

In our FastPass module, get_time/1 extracts the time value from a FastPass and implements eq_time/0 using contramap/1, so equality is based on time.

lib/fun_park/fast_pass.ex
```
def get_time(%__MODULE__{time: time}), do: time

def eq_time do
  Eq.Utils.contramap(&get_time/1)
end
```

Now, if we want to compare two FastPass values by time, we can use eq_time.

## Run It

Create the Rides:

```
iex> mansion = FunPark.Ride.make("Dark Mansion", min_age: 14, tags: [:dark])
iex> tea_cup = FunPark.Ride.make("Tea Cup")
```

Generate a FastPass for the Dark Mansion:

```
iex> datetime = DateTime.new!(~D[2025-06-01], ~T[13:00:00])

iex> fast_pass_a = FunPark.FastPass.make(mansion, datetime)
%FunPark.FastPass{
  id: 3618,
  ride: %FunPark.Ride{
    id: 3490,
    name: "Dark Mansion",
    ...
  },
  time: ~U[2025-06-01 13:00:00Z]
}
```

Generate another FastPass for the Tea Cup using the same time:

```
iex> fast_pass_b = FunPark.FastPass.make(tea_cup, datetime)
%FunPark.FastPass{
  id: 3650,
  ride: %FunPark.Ride{
    id: 3522,
    name: "Tea Cup",
    ...
  },
  time: ~U[2025-06-01 13:00:00Z]
}
```

Our default equality check knows these are different (they have different IDs):

```
iex> FunPark.Eq.eq?(fast_pass_a, fast_pass_b)
false
```

But our new custom equality knows they have the same time:

```
iex> FunPark.FastPass.eq_time.eq?.(fast_pass_a, fast_pass_b)
true
```

## You're Gonna Need a Bigger Boat

Sometimes our tools aren't big enough to handle what's lurking beneath.

Let's take a closer look at our current contramap/1 function:

```
def contramap(f) do
  %{
    eq?: fn a, b -> Eq.eq?(f.(a), f.(b)) end,
    not_eq?: fn a, b -> Eq.not_eq?(f.(a), f.(b)) end
  }
end
```

In Elixir, protocols are tied to named modules. Our custom Eq instance, derived in contramap/1, isn't associated with any particular module, so we store its comparison functions in a map.

Because Elixir calls functions differently depending on where they're stored—implicitly for modules and explicitly for maps—we can't treat them interchangeably. To keep things composable and consistent, our best option is to normalize everything to maps. (The code is on the next page.)

```
lib/fun_park/eq/utils.ex
def to_eq_map(%{eq?: eq_fun, not_eq?: not_eq_fun} = eq_map)
    when is_function(eq_fun, 2) and is_function(not_eq_fun, 2) do
  eq_map
end

def to_eq_map(module) when is_atom(module) do
  %{
    eq?: &module.eq?/2,
    not_eq?: &module.not_eq?/2
  }
end
```

The to_eq_map/1 function ensures that we always work with a map representation of equality checks. If we pass a map that has eq? and not_eq? functions, it's returned as-is. If we pass in a module, it extracts the corresponding functions and wraps them in a map, standardizing our interface.

Here's an improved contramap/1 function using this approach:

```
lib/fun_park/eq/utils.ex
def contramap(f, eq \\ Eq) do
  eq = to_eq_map(eq)

  %{
    eq?: fn a, b -> eq.eq?.(f.(a), f.(b)) end,
    not_eq?: fn a, b -> eq.not_eq?.(f.(a), f.(b)) end
  }
end
```

Not only have we standardized the representation, but eq \\ Eq preserves the default while still allowing us to swap in custom equality logic.

This is a bigger—much more composable—boat.

## Simplify Equality Checks

Even though we've standardized our internal logic around the map-based representation of Eq, usage still differs depending on whether it's produced by the protocol or by contramap/2. From the caller's perspective, that distinction is an internal detail. Let's introduce a single eq?/2 function to fold that difference into a unified interface.

```
lib/fun_park/eq/utils.ex
def eq?(a, b, eq \\ Eq) do
  eq = to_eq_map(eq)
  eq.eq?.(a, b)
end
```

Now, callers have a single entry point that uses the protocol by default but still allows custom equality logic to be passed in as an optional parameter.

This keeps comparison logic adaptable without changing the underlying data, helping the system stay flexible as it evolves.

### Run It

Let's regenerate our passes:

```
iex> mansion = FunPark.Ride.make("Dark Mansion", min_age: 14, tags: [:dark])
iex> tea_cup = FunPark.Ride.make("Tea Cup")

iex> datetime = DateTime.new!(~D[2025-06-01], ~T[13:00:00])

iex> fast_pass_a = FunPark.FastPass.make(mansion, datetime)
iex> fast_pass_b = FunPark.FastPass.make(tea_cup, datetime)
```

From the context of FastPass, the passes have different IDs, so they are different:

```
iex> FunPark.Eq.Utils.eq?(fast_pass_a, fast_pass_b)
false
```

But we can inject our eq_time/0 logic to determine they're scheduled for the same time:

```
iex> has_eq_time = FunPark.FastPass.eq_time()
iex> FunPark.Eq.Utils.eq?(fast_pass_a, fast_pass_b, has_eq_time)
true
```

We've structured equality around domain context—using protocols for shared behavior and contramap to adapt comparisons to specific needs, making the system easier to use and evolve.

## Harness Equality for Collections

Since we've abstracted equality with the Eq protocol, we can define context-aware versions of common list operations like deduplication, intersection, and subset checks.

| Operation | Description |
| --- | --- |
| uniq/2 | Remove duplicates. |
| union/3 | Combine unique elements. |
| intersection/3 | Find common elements. |
| difference/3 | Exclude elements in second list. |
| symmetric_difference/3 | Elements in either, but not both. |
| subset?/3 | Check if all elements exist in another list. |
| superset?/3 | Check if one list contains all elements of another. |

## Unique

FunPark tracks the number of patrons entering per day, but some patrons leave and reenter, so we need a unique count.

lib/fun_park/list.ex
```elixir
def uniq(list, eq \\ FunPark.Eq) when is_list(list) do
  list
  |> Enum.reduce([], fn item, acc ->
    if Enum.any?(acc, &Eq.Utils.eq?(item, &1, eq)),
      do: acc,
      else: [item | acc]
  end)
  |> :lists.reverse()
end
```

First, let's make two copies of Alice:

```elixir
iex> alice_a = FunPark.Patron.make("Alice", 15, 50)
%FunPark.Patron{
  id: 2,
  name: "Alice",
  ticket_tier: :basic,
  ...
}

iex> alice_b = FunPark.Patron.change(alice_a, %{ticket_tier: :premium})
%FunPark.Patron{
  id: 2,
  name: "Alice",
  ticket_tier: :premium,
  ...
}

iex> FunPark.List.uniq([alice_a, alice_b])
[
  %FunPark.Patron{
    id: 2,
    name: "Alice",
    ticket_tier: :basic,
    ...
  }
]
```

Even though alice_a and alice_b have different ticket tiers, they share the same ID. Since uniq/1 is context-aware, it used the Eq implementation for Patron and removed the second entry.

## Union

FunPark tracks ride downtime from multiple sources, including scheduled maintenance and unexpected breakdowns. At the end of the day, we need to combine these logs to generate a unique list of rides that were offline.

We can compose union/3 using uniq/2:

```
lib/fun_park/list.ex
def union(list1, list2, eq \\ FunPark.Eq)
    when is_list(list1) and is_list(list2) do
  (list1 ++ list2) |> uniq(eq)
end
```

Again, since union/3 is context-aware, it knows how to manage a list of rides.

```
iex> tea_cup = FunPark.Ride.make("Tea Cup")
iex> haunted_mansion = FunPark.Ride.make("Haunted Mansion")
iex> apple_cart = FunPark.Ride.make("Apple Cart")

iex> maintenance_log = [haunted_mansion, apple_cart]
iex> breakdown_log = [tea_cup, haunted_mansion]

iex> FunPark.List.union(maintenance_log, breakdown_log)
[
  %FunPark.Ride{name: "Haunted Mansion", ...},
  %FunPark.Ride{name: "Apple Cart", ...},
  %FunPark.Ride{name: "Tea Cup", ...}
]
```

This combines both lists into one, removing duplicates based on the Ride's Eq implementation.

## Intersection

FunPark adjusts incentives to balance crowd flow, steering guests away from overbooked rides. By intersecting rides with the longest wait times and rides with the most FastPass bookings, we identify high-demand attractions.

intersection/3 can be composed from uniq/2:

```
lib/fun_park/list.ex
def intersection(list1, list2, eq \\ FunPark.Eq)
    when is_list(list1) and is_list(list2) do
  list1
  |> Enum.filter(fn item ->
    Enum.any?(list2, &Eq.Utils.eq?(item, &1, eq))
  end)
  |> uniq(eq)
end
```

The Haunted Mansion is in high demand:

```
iex> long_wait = [haunted_mansion, apple_cart]
iex> most_fast_pass = [tea_cup, haunted_mansion]
iex> FunPark.List.intersection(long_wait, most_fast_pass)
[
  %FunPark.Ride{name: "Haunted Mansion", ...}
]
```

## Difference

Not all rides in FunPark are accessible to every patron. We can use difference to subtract restricted rides from the full list, identifying attractions available to all guests.

lib/fun_park/list.ex
```
def difference(list1, list2, eq \\ FunPark.Eq)
    when is_list(list1) and is_list(list2) do
  list1
  |> Enum.reject(fn item ->
    Enum.any?(list2, &Eq.Utils.eq?(item, &1, eq))
  end)
  |> uniq(eq)
end
```

Apple Cart is available to everyone:

```
iex> all_rides = [haunted_mansion, apple_cart]
iex> restricted_rides = [haunted_mansion]
iex> FunPark.List.difference(all_rides, restricted_rides)
[
  %FunPark.Ride{name: "Apple Cart", ...}
]
```

## Symmetric Difference

To evaluate whether our FastPass strategy is working, we need to find rides that don't behave as expected. High wait times should correlate with FastPass usage, so rides that appear in only one of the two lists are outliers, and they need to be investigated. This is *symmetric difference*: the set of elements that appear in either list but not both.

We can compose symmetric_difference/3 from difference/3 and uniq/2:

```
lib/fun_park/list.ex
def symmetric_difference(list1, list2, eq \\ FunPark.Eq)
    when is_list(list1) and is_list(list2) do
  (difference(list1, list2, eq) ++
     difference(list2, list1, eq))
  |> uniq(eq)
end
```

Apple Cart and Tea Cup appear in only one of the two lists, which means they aren't behaving as expected:

```
iex> long_wait_times = [haunted_mansion, apple_cart]
iex> fast_pass_usage = [tea_cup, haunted_mansion]

iex> FunPark.List.symmetric_difference(
  long_wait_times,
  fast_pass_usage
)
[
  %FunPark.Ride{name: "Apple Cart", ...},
  %FunPark.Ride{name: "Tea Cup", ...}
]
```

## Subset

FunPark needs to track if guests made full use of their FastPasses. We can check if every eligible ride was used by verifying that the patron's FastPass list is a subset of the rides they rode.

Here, we use Eq with Elixir's Enum.all/2 and Enum.any/2 to check if the first list is a subset of the second:

```
lib/fun_park/list.ex
def subset?(small, large, eq \\ FunPark.Eq)
    when is_list(small) and is_list(large) do
  Enum.all?(small, fn item ->
    Enum.any?(large, &Eq.Utils.eq?(item, &1, eq))
  end)
end
```

We find that our patron has indeed completed all of their FastPass rides:

```
fast_pass_rides = [tea_cup, banana_slip]
rides_completed = [haunted_mansion, tea_cup, banana_slip]

iex> FunPark.List.subset?(fast_pass_rides, rides_completed)
true
```

## Superset

FunPark looks for engagement, upgrade, or access opportunities by tracking when guests take rides when they didn't have a FastPass.

We can compose superset?/3 from subset?/3:

```
lib/fun_park/list.ex
def superset?(large, small, eq \\ FunPark.Eq)
    when is_list(small) and is_list(large) do
  subset?(small, large, eq)
end
```

This patron rode more than just their FastPass attractions:

```
fast_pass_rides = [haunted_mansion]
rides_completed = [tea_cup, banana_slip, haunted_mansion]

iex> FunPark.List.superset?(rides_completed, fast_pass_rides)
true
```

Composing with Eq gives us higher-level operations that are easier to reuse, reason about, and adapt to changes in our domain as it evolves.

## Act on It

Spend some time tinkering with equality. Try out the collection functions using simple values like numbers or atoms to get familiar with how they work.

Create a contramap/1 that normalizes strings before comparing them—make sure they're trimmed and use the same case.

A patron wants to give their FastPasses to a friend. Before transferring, how would you check that none of the friend's passes are for the same time?

Find the Equality Chapter Answers, on page 209.

# What You've Learned

Equality isn't just a basic comparison—it reflects the rules of the domain. For patrons, rides, or FastPasses, *equal* means what the business says it means.

With the Eq protocol, we made those rules explicit and reusable—not just for direct comparisons but for higher-level operations like uniq, intersection, and difference.

By centralizing equality logic, we avoid duplication and drift. And because those rules live close to the domain, they're easy to update as our understanding grows—ensuring that consistent, correct behavior follows throughout the system.

That's the shift: from ad-hoc checks to a composable structure that stays flexible as the domain evolves. In the next chapter, we'll build on this with Ord—capturing not just when things are equal but how they relate.

If this is your first time working with protocols, take time to practice. Define equality for a new domain and work through the edge cases. Use the iex session or Livebooks to gather feedback.[2] Or spend some time arguing with the LLM Tutor.[3]

Deliberate practice is hard, but it pays off.

---

2. https://www.funxlib.com/book-livebooks.html
3. https://www.funxlib.com/tutor.html

# CHAPTER 3

# Create Flexible Ordering with Protocols

> A production-ready Ord is available in the Funx library.[1]

We often need to compare things—not just check if they're the same but decide which comes first. Should patrons be ranked by loyalty tier or reward points? Should rides be sorted by name, wait time, or thrill factor?

With Eq, we made equality explicit and reusable. Now we'll define ordering in the same spirit, using Elixir's protocol system to express comparison logic that reflects domain meaning.

Order builds on equality. If we can tell which of two things comes first, we can also tell if they're equal. Equality is binary—it's either true or false. Order gives us three outcomes: less than, equal, or greater. In a typed language, we'd say Ord extends Eq. In Elixir, protocols are independent, so that relationship is informal.

Like equality, ordering has rules:

- *Reflexivity:* $a \leq a$.
- *Antisymmetry:* If $a \leq b$ and $b \leq a$, then $a = b$.
- *Transitivity:* If $a \leq b$ and $b \leq c$, then $a \leq c$.

Once we internalize what it means for one thing to come before another, we begin to see beyond basic sorting. Priority queues, deduplication windows, and algorithms such as Dijkstra's all rely on order.

---

1.   https://hexdocs.pm/funx/Funx.Ord.html

As with Eq, we'll use projection and delegation to define order at the core of the domain—composable, testable, and easy to update when the rules change. Let's get started.

## Define Order with a Protocol

The Ord protocol defines functions that mirror Elixir's built-in ordering operators, allowing us to express domain-specific comparisons.

lib/fun_park/ord.ex
```
defprotocol FunPark.Ord do
  @fallback_to_any true

  def lt?(a, b)
  def le?(a, b)
  def gt?(a, b)
  def ge?(a, b)
end
```

Elixir protocols do not include default implementations, but @fallback_to_any lets us specify a generic fallback when no type-specific implementation is defined.

> **Joe asks:**
> ## Wait, Can't You Just Derive Most of Those?
>
> Yes—like our Eq protocol, when implementing the Ord protocol, you're free to define lt?/2 and derive the rest. Elixir is eager, so while the cost of deriving is small, it's not free—especially with complex orderings over large lists. By defining all four (lt?, le?, gt?, ge?) in the protocol, I'm deferring that decision to the implementer.

lib/fun_park/ord.ex
```
defimpl FunPark.Ord, for: Any do
  def lt?(a, b), do: a < b
  def le?(a, b), do: a <= b
  def gt?(a, b), do: a > b
  def ge?(a, b), do: a >= b
end
```

The Any implementation delegates directly to Elixir's native comparison operators, allowing FunPark.Ord to work with any type that supports built-in comparison.

## Run It

Start Elixir's iex shell and run the mix script to compile the code and load the project.

```
iex -S mix
```

Using Elixir's operators, we see that 1 is less than 2:

```
iex> 1 < 2
true
iex> 1 > 2
false
```

Our Ord implementation produces the same results:

```
iex> FunPark.Ord.lt?(1, 2)
true
iex> FunPark.Ord.gt?(1, 2)
false
```

Like Eq, we can now create context-aware Ord.

# Implement Order for FunPark Contexts

With Eq, we used id as the default—but for Ord, we'll base comparisons on what matters in each case: name for rides and patrons, and time for FastPasses.

## Ride Context

After talking with our Ride expert, we've confirmed that the default ordering for rides should be based on name.

lib/fun_park/ride.ex
```
defimpl FunPark.Ord, for: FunPark.Ride do
  alias FunPark.Ord
  alias FunPark.Ride

  def lt?(%Ride{name: v1}, %Ride{name: v2}), do: Ord.lt?(v1, v2)
  def le?(%Ride{name: v1}, %Ride{name: v2}), do: Ord.le?(v1, v2)
  def gt?(%Ride{name: v1}, %Ride{name: v2}), do: Ord.gt?(v1, v2)
  def ge?(%Ride{name: v1}, %Ride{name: v2}), do: Ord.ge?(v1, v2)
end
```

This extracts the name field from each Ride and delegates comparison to the Ord protocol. This is *projection*: mapping a complex structure to a simpler one before applying logic.

## Run It

First, let's make a couple of rides:

```
iex> banana_slip = FunPark.Ride.make("Banana Slip")
%FunPark.Ride{
  id: 3524,
  name: "Banana Slip",
  ...
}
iex> apple_cart = FunPark.Ride.make("Apple Cart")
%FunPark.Ride{
  id: 3556,
  name: "Apple Cart",
  ...
}
```

In this case, Elixir's built-in < operator sorts Apple Cart *after* Banana Slip:

```
iex> apple_cart < banana_slip
false
```

That's because Elixir compares structs as maps, using their keys in alphabetical order. In Ride, the first differing key is id. Here, Banana Slip's id happens to come before Apple Cart's, so Elixir compares those values and never reaches the name.

Keep in mind that our id values are autogenerated by Erlang, and their order is unpredictable. In one run, the id might be greater; in another, it might be smaller.

In contrast, our Ord protocol knows that Ride values should be compared by name:

```
iex> FunPark.Ord.lt?(apple_cart, banana_slip)
true
```

## FastPass Context

Our FastPass expert has identified time as the default field for comparisons—passes should be ordered with the earliest time first.

```
lib/fun_park/fast_pass.ex
defimpl FunPark.Ord, for: FunPark.FastPass do
  alias FunPark.Ord
  alias FunPark.FastPass

  def lt?(%FastPass{time: v1}, %FastPass{time: v2}), do: Ord.lt?(v1, v2)
  def le?(%FastPass{time: v1}, %FastPass{time: v2}), do: Ord.le?(v1, v2)
```

```
    def gt?(%FastPass{time: v1}, %FastPass{time: v2}), do: Ord.gt?(v1, v2)
    def ge?(%FastPass{time: v1}, %FastPass{time: v2}), do: Ord.ge?(v1, v2)
end
```

But not so fast—DateTime is just a struct. It falls back to Elixir's default comparison, which doesn't account for temporal order.

## Run It

Let's create a couple of timestamps to illustrate the problem:

```
iex> datetime_1 = DateTime.new!(~D[2025-06-01], ~T[13:10:00.000005])
iex> datetime_2 = DateTime.new!(~D[2025-06-01], ~T[13:40:00.000004])
```

The first comes before the second, so it should be less—but it's not:

```
iex> datetime_1 < datetime_2
false
```

That's because Elixir's < compares struct fields in alphabetical order. Since :microsecond comes before :minute, it compares 5 > 4 and returns false even though the actual time is earlier.

DateTime.compare/2, on the other hand, does understand time:

```
iex> DateTime.compare(datetime_1, datetime_2)
:lt
```

We can implement our own Ord instance for DateTime with its compare/2 function:

```
lib/fun_park/ord.ex
defimpl FunPark.Ord, for: DateTime do
  def lt?(a, b), do: DateTime.compare(a, b) == :lt
  def le?(a, b), do: match?(x when x in [:lt, :eq], DateTime.compare(a, b))
  def gt?(a, b), do: DateTime.compare(a, b) == :gt
  def ge?(a, b), do: match?(x when x in [:gt, :eq], DateTime.compare(a, b))
end
```

We've added a new Ord instance for DateTime, and because FastPass uses projection, we don't need to change its implementation. Once DateTime has its own Ord instance, comparisons just work—resolving without falling back to Any. This is composability through delegation: new behavior can be inserted without touching existing code.

### Run It

Let's start with a couple of FastPasses:

```
iex> apple_cart = FunPark.Ride.make("Apple Cart")
iex> banana_slip = FunPark.Ride.make("Banana Slip")

iex> datetime_1 = DateTime.new!(~D[2025-06-01], ~T[13:10:00.000005])
iex> datetime_2 = DateTime.new!(~D[2025-06-01], ~T[13:40:00.000004])

iex> fast_pass_1 = FunPark.FastPass.make(banana_slip, datetime_1)
iex> fast_pass_2 = FunPark.FastPass.make(apple_cart, datetime_2)
```

Our default Ord correctly identifies that the first pass comes before the second:

```
iex> FunPark.Ord.lt?(fast_pass_1, fast_pass_2)
true
```

Let's update fast_pass_1 to a later time:

```
iex> time_3 = DateTime.new!(~D[2025-06-01], ~T[15:00:00.000012])
iex> fast_pass_1 = FunPark.FastPass.change(fast_pass_1, %{time: time_3})
```

The first pass is now considered greater:

```
iex> FunPark.Ord.gt?(fast_pass_1, fast_pass_2)
true
```

### Patron Context

Our Patron expert confirmed that the default sort is by name, but in some cases patrons need to be sorted by ticket tier instead. We can implement this new, non-default logic using a contravariant functor, just like Transform Inputs Before Matching, on page 17.

## Transform Inputs Before Comparison

Let's define a contramap/1 in the Ord.Utils module:

lib/fun_park/ord/utils.ex
```
def contramap(f, ord \\ Ord) do
  ord = to_ord_map(ord)

  %{
    lt?: fn a, b -> ord.lt?.(f.(a), f.(b)) end,
    le?: fn a, b -> ord.le?.(f.(a), f.(b)) end,
    gt?: fn a, b -> ord.gt?.(f.(a), f.(b)) end,
    ge?: fn a, b -> ord.ge?.(f.(a), f.(b)) end
  }
end
```

```
lib/fun_park/ord/utils.ex
def to_ord_map(%{lt?: lt_f, le?: le_f, gt?: gt_f, ge?: ge_f} = ord_map)
    when is_function(lt_f, 2) and
           is_function(le_f, 2) and
           is_function(gt_f, 2) and
           is_function(ge_f, 2),
    do: ord_map

def to_ord_map(module) when is_atom(module) do
  %{
    lt?: &module.lt?/2,
    le?: &module.le?/2,
    gt?: &module.gt?/2,
    ge?: &module.ge?/2
  }
end
```

As with Eq, our Ord contramap needs to extract and store the comparison functions in a map, resulting in two representations: protocol-based and map-based. To keep things consistent, we use to_ord_map/1 to normalize everything to a unified, map-based form.

Our Patron expert tells us that ticket tiers should be sorted in a specific order: :basic, :premium, :vip. While these atoms happen to sort correctly, that's an implementation detail—not a rule we want to rely on. Instead, we use con-tramap/1 to explicitly project each tier to an integer—:basic → 1, :premium → 2, :vip → 3—and let Elixir's built-in integer comparisons handle the sort.

```
lib/fun_park/patron.ex
defp tier_priority(:vip), do: 3
defp tier_priority(:premium), do: 2
defp tier_priority(:basic), do: 1
defp tier_priority(_), do: 0

defp get_ticket_tier_priority(%__MODULE__{ticket_tier: ticket_tier}),
  do: tier_priority(ticket_tier)

def ord_by_ticket_tier do
  Ord.Utils.contramap(&get_ticket_tier_priority/1)
end
```

### Joe asks:
### Doesn't This Change the Ticket Tier Value?

If you're like me, the first time you encountered contramap, you might have assumed it changes the original data—but it doesn't. Instead, contramap projects the data into a simpler form for comparison. The original structure remains untouched—only the comparison logic changes.

## Run It

Let's start with two patrons with differing ticket tiers:

```
iex> alice = FunPark.Patron.make("Alice", 15, 50, ticket_tier: :premium)
%FunPark.Patron{
  id: 1666,
  name: "Alice",
  ticket_tier: :premium,
  ...
}
iex> beth = FunPark.Patron.make("Beth", 16, 53)
%FunPark.Patron{
  id: 1698,
  name: "Beth",
  ticket_tier: :basic,
  ...
}
```

Alice ranks higher than Beth due to her :premium ticket:

```
iex> ticket_ord = FunPark.Patron.ord_by_ticket_tier()

iex> ticket_ord.gt?.(alice, beth)
true
```

Later, Beth decides to upgrade to :vip:

```
iex> beth = FunPark.Patron.change(beth, %{ticket_tier: :vip})
%FunPark.Patron{
  id: 1698,
  name: "Beth",
  ticket_tier: :vip,
  ...
}
```

With a :vip ticket, Beth now ranks higher than Alice:

```
iex> ticket_ord.gt?.(beth, alice)
true
```

By anchoring ordering to domain meaning, our comparisons express intent—making logic clearer, more consistent, and easier to evolve.

## Act on It

Our Patron expert wants to prioritize service for certain guests. Start by creating an ordering based on reward points. Patrons with more points should be considered greater.

Meanwhile, our Ride expert is working on a suggestion engine and needs rides sorted by current wait time. Rides with shorter waits should be considered less.

Use contramap/1 to define the ordering logic for each case, and try swapping in different fields to see how it affects comparisons.

Find the Order Chapter Answers, on page 210.

# Harness Order for Collections

Ordering logic often ends up at the edges of a codebase—buried in list views, helper functions, or last-minute controller tweaks. It's typically written as a one-off, overly specific function, then copied and pasted across the system. Our goal is to move Ord back to the core, where it can evolve with the domain.

## Single-Purpose Sorting

Our Ride expert needs the Park's electronic maps to show rides sorted alphabetically by name.

Let's start with a typical sort by name for a list of rides.

```
def sort_rides(rides) do
  Enum.sort(rides, fn ride1, ride2 -> ride1.name < ride2.name end)
end
```

## Run It

Now we can create a couple of rides and sort them:

```
iex> apple_cart = FunPark.Ride.make("Apple Cart")
iex> banana_slip = FunPark.Ride.make("Banana Slip")

iex> FunPark.List.sort_rides([banana_slip, apple_cart])
[
  %FunPark.Ride{ name: "Apple Cart", ... },
  %FunPark.Ride{ name: "Banana Slip", ...}
]
```

While sort_rides/1 works, it locks the sorting logic into a single, specific case. Left as is, this kind of approach tends to sprawl, risking inconsistency and making future changes harder to manage. Let's leverage our Ord protocol to extract the reusable logic.

## Generalize the Sort

First, we can simplify things by implementing a compare/2 function that translates the Ord protocol into a familiar form: less than, equal to, or greater than. In many languages, this is represented as -1, 0, or 1, but as we saw with DateTime, Elixir uses the atoms :lt, :eq, and :gt.

lib/fun_park/ord/utils.ex
```
def compare(a, b, ord \\ Ord) do
  ord = to_ord_map(ord)

  cond do
    ord.lt?.(a, b) -> :lt
    ord.gt?.(a, b) -> :gt
    true -> :eq
  end
end
```

Our compare/2 function folds both representations of Ord logic—protocol-based (implicit) and map-based (explicit)—into a single interface, so callers don't need to worry about which form is being used. And rather than relying on Boolean operators to check if one value is less than or greater than another, we cut to the chase, describing the relationship directly with :lt, :eq, or :gt.

We can compare simple values:

```
iex> FunPark.Ord.Utils.compare(1, 1)
:eq
iex> FunPark.Ord.Utils.compare(1, 2)
:lt
iex> FunPark.Ord.Utils.compare(1, 0)
:gt
```

We can also compare context-aware values, such as ride:

```
iex> apple_cart = FunPark.Ride.make("Apple Cart")
iex> banana_slip = FunPark.Ride.make("Banana Slip")

iex> FunPark.Ord.Utils.compare(apple_cart, apple_cart)
:eq
iex> FunPark.Ord.Utils.compare(apple_cart, banana_slip)
:lt
iex> FunPark.Ord.Utils.compare(banana_slip, apple_cart)
:gt
```

Languages like JavaScript and Python include a comparator for sorting lists. Elixir does not, but we can define one using compare/2.

lib/fun_park/ord/utils.ex
```
def comparator(ord_module) do
  fn a, b -> compare(a, b, ord_module) != :gt end
end
```

When sorting, using not :gt is preferable to :lt because it ensures a *stable sort*, where elements considered equal retain their original relative positions.

Finally, let's implement our own generic List.sort/2, leveraging comparator/1 with Elixir's Enum.sort/2:

```
lib/fun_park/list.ex
def sort(list, ord \\ FunPark.Ord) when is_list(list) do
  Enum.sort(list, Ord.Utils.comparator(ord))
end
```

This gives us flexible, context-aware sorting for both primitives and our domain-specific types, leveraging Elixir's polymorphism to adapt behavior based on input context.

We can sort simple values:

```
iex> FunPark.List.sort([:banana, :pear, :apple])
[:apple, :banana, :pear]
```

Or we can sort context-aware values that have implemented the Ord protocol:

```
iex> banana_slip = FunPark.Ride.make("Banana Slip")
iex> apple_cart = FunPark.Ride.make("Apple Cart")

iex> FunPark.List.sort([banana_slip, apple_cart])
[
  %FunPark.Ride{name: "Apple Cart", ... },
  %FunPark.Ride{name: "Banana Slip", ... }
]
```

To generate our Ride expert's report, we didn't need a one-off, we just needed List.sort/1.

## Strict Sort

Our Ride expert also needs an operational snapshot of current wait times across the park. They don't need the full list, just a summary of the unique wait times being reported, sorted from shortest to longest.

A *strict sort* returns a sorted list of unique values. We can build this by composing our existing uniq/2 and sort/2 functions.

### Houston, We Have a Problem

A strict sort only works when Eq and Ord are aligned. But our Ride struct follows the entity pattern: equality is based on ride ID, while ordering is based on a different field. So if we try to deduplicate using Eq, we'll get identity-based uniqueness, not value-based.

To resolve this, we need a way to derive an Eq instance from an Ord instance—one that defines equality in terms of ordering:

lib/fun_park/ord/utils.ex
```
def to_eq(ord \\ Ord) do
  %{
    eq?: fn a, b -> compare(a, b, ord) == :eq end,
    not_eq?: fn a, b -> compare(a, b, ord) != :eq end
  }
end
```

Now we can define strict_sort/2 by composing uniq/2 and sort/2, using to_eq/1 to ensure both steps share the same logic:

lib/fun_park/list.ex
```
def strict_sort(list, ord \\ FunPark.Ord) when is_list(list) do
  list
  |> uniq(Ord.Utils.to_eq(ord))
  |> sort(ord)
end
```

Our strict_sort/2 function works on simple values, like atoms:

```
iex> FunPark.List.strict_sort([:banana, :orange, :banana, :apple])
[:apple, :banana, :orange]
```

It also handles structures that implement the Ord protocol, such as Ride.

Let's create a few rides:

```
iex> tea_cup = FunPark.Ride.make("Tea Cup", wait_time: 40)
iex> haunted_mansion = FunPark.Ride.make("Haunted Mansion", wait_time: 20)
iex> river_ride = FunPark.Ride.make("River Ride", wait_time: 40)
iex> rides = [tea_cup, haunted_mansion, river_ride]
```

Using ord_by_wait_time/0, we can sort rides by their current wait times:

```
iex> ord_wait_time = FunPark.Ride.ord_by_wait_time()
iex> FunPark.List.sort(rides, ord_wait_time)
[
  %FunPark.Ride{ name: "Haunted Mansion", wait_time: 20, ... },
  %FunPark.Ride{ name: "Tea Cup", wait_time: 40, ... },
  %FunPark.Ride{ name: "River Ride", wait_time: 40, ... }
]
```

To generate our Ride expert's snapshot—just one ride per distinct wait time—we use strict_sort/2:

```
iex> FunPark.List.strict_sort(rides, ord_wait_time)
[
  %FunPark.Ride{ name: "Haunted Mansion", wait_time: 20, ... },
  %FunPark.Ride{ name: "Tea Cup", wait_time: 40, ... }
]
```

Now we have a deduplicated snapshot of the unique wait times currently reported across the park.

## Reverse the Order

Sometimes we need to sort in reverse. While we could sort first and then call Enum.reverse/1, it's more efficient to invert the Ord logic directly, avoiding the extra pass through the data.

The reverse/1 function returns a new Ord with the comparison logic flipped:

lib/fun_park/ord/utils.ex
```
def reverse(ord \\ Ord) do
  ord = to_ord_map(ord)

  %{
    lt?: ord.gt?,
    le?: ord.ge?,
    gt?: ord.lt?,
    ge?: ord.le?
  }
end
```

### Run It

We can invert the result of compare/3:

```
iex> reverse_ord = FunPark.Ord.Utils.reverse()

iex> FunPark.Ord.Utils.compare(:apple, :banana)
:lt

iex> FunPark.Ord.Utils.compare(:apple, :banana, reverse_ord)
:gt
```

By default, Patron sorts by name, so Alice comes before Beth:

```
iex> alice = FunPark.Patron.make("Alice", 14, 140, ticket_tier: :vip)
iex> beth = FunPark.Patron.make("Beth", 15, 130, ticket_tier: :premium)

iex> FunPark.List.sort([alice, beth])
[
  %FunPark.Patron{ name: "Alice", ... },
  %FunPark.Patron{ name: "Beth", ... }
]
```

With reverse/0, Beth now comes before Alice:

```
iex> reverse_ord = FunPark.Ord.Utils.reverse()
iex> FunPark.List.sort([alice, beth], reverse_ord)
[
  %FunPark.Patron{ name: "Beth", ... },
  %FunPark.Patron{ name: "Alice", ... }
]
```

Reverse can also be composed with other Ord logic.

For example, if we sort by ticket tier, Alice's VIP ticket comes after Beth's Premium:

```
iex> ticket_ord = FunPark.Patron.ord_by_ticket_tier()
iex> FunPark.List.sort([alice, beth], ticket_ord)
[
  %FunPark.Patron{ name: "Beth", ticket_tier: :premium, ... },
  %FunPark.Patron{ name: "Alice", ticket_tier: :vip, ... }
]
```

And with reverse/1, we can invert the logic so higher ticket tiers come first:

```
iex> reverse_ticket_ord = FunPark.Ord.Utils.reverse(ticket_ord)
iex> FunPark.List.sort([alice, beth], reverse_ticket_ord)
[
  %FunPark.Patron{ name: "Alice", ticket_tier: :vip, ... },
  %FunPark.Patron{ name: "Beth", ticket_tier: :premium, ... }
]
```

Naive sorts often involve multiple steps, each pass reprocessing the list. But as reverse/1 shows, we don't need to rewrite the data—we can rewrite the rules!

# Reduce Repetitive Code with Macros

Our Eq and Ord implementations are mostly boilerplate, which introduces the "copy-paste" (or "copy-pasta") problem, where repetitive code increases the likelihood of errors due to oversight.

Instead of manually implementing Ord for every struct, we can automate our typical use case with a macro.

lib/fun_park/macros.ex
```elixir
defmacro ord_for(for_struct, field) do
  quote do
    alias FunPark.Ord

    defimpl FunPark.Ord, for: unquote(for_struct) do
      def lt?(
            %unquote(for_struct){unquote(field) => v1},
            %unquote(for_struct){unquote(field) => v2}
          ),
          do: Ord.lt?(v1, v2)

      def le?(
            %unquote(for_struct){unquote(field) => v1},
            %unquote(for_struct){unquote(field) => v2}
          ),
          do: Ord.le?(v1, v2)

      def gt?(
            %unquote(for_struct){unquote(field) => v1},
            %unquote(for_struct){unquote(field) => v2}
          ),
          do: Ord.gt?(v1, v2)

      def ge?(
            %unquote(for_struct){unquote(field) => v1},
            %unquote(for_struct){unquote(field) => v2}
          ),
          do: Ord.ge?(v1, v2)
    end
  end
end
```

For Patron we would implement this:

lib/fun_park/patron.ex
```elixir
ord_for(FunPark.Patron, :name)
```

## Act on It

Experiment with contramap/1 and reverse/1 to refine ordering logic further. For example, how would you sort patrons with the most reward points first?

Try implementing other abstractions for Ord, such as these:

- min/2 and max/2—return the smallest or largest value based on a given Ord implementation.
- Create a macro to implement Eq.

Find the Order Chapter Answers, on page 210.

# What You've Learned

Ord is more than a way to check whether one thing comes before another—it's a way to make ordering logic explicit, reusable, and shaped by domain context. Whether sorting patrons by tier or rides by name, we're not just comparing, we're expressing intent.

Instead of hardcoding comparisons throughout the system, we've built a flexible framework that adapts to each use case. By centralizing that logic, we avoid duplication and drift—and when requirements change, we update in one place and trust the new behavior to apply consistently.

Elixir doesn't give us static types, but we get similar structure through pattern matching and protocols. By projecting to simpler forms and delegating through protocol dispatch, we get composable, context-aware ordering, defined at the core of the domain, not scattered at the edges.

Even if you go no further, you now have the tools to define comparison behavior that's consistent, reusable, and tailored to your domain—a way to make behavior explicit and easier to update as your team's understanding of the domain evolves.

What if we want to sort by ticket tier *then* reward points? Earlier, we saw how reverse/1 let us change the sort order by rewriting the rules. We can take that idea further: instead of chaining multiple sort passes, we can combine the logic into a single Ord. In the next chapter, we'll introduce the tool that specializes in combining things: the monoid.

Stop and ask yourself hard questions. Do you really understand contramap/1? Expert knowledge doesn't come from passive reading; it comes from refining and extending mental models. Don't move on from ideas you only *sort of* understand. Pause and dig in.

This book isn't a tutorial or a cookbook. It's here to help you build intuition, and that only happens when you try things on your own terms.

# CHAPTER 4

# Combine with Monoids

A production-ready Monoid is available in the Funx library.[1]

Who gets priority—a guest with lots of reward points, someone with a FastPass, a VIP, or a rider with accessibility needs? What looks like a comparison problem is a combination problem.

With Eq, we made equality explicit: a rule for when two things are equal. With Ord, we gave structure to comparisons, ensuring ordering stays predictable. With *monoids*, we make combination explicit: a reusable abstraction instead of an ad-hoc operation.

You already use monoids: adding numbers, multiplying values, reducing a list. The operations vary, but the mental model—identity and combination—remains constant. That pattern also shows up in surprisingly sophisticated places: parallel aggregations, undo/redo systems, conflict-free replicated data types (CRDTs).

To understand why monoids work, we need to look at the rules that make them reliable.

A *semigroup* defines how elements combine and must satisfy two rules:

- *Associativity:* Grouping doesn't change the result—a ⊕ (b ⊕ c) = (a ⊕ b) ⊕ c.
- *Closure:* Combining two elements produces another element of the same kind.

---

1.   https://hexdocs.pm/funx/Funx.Monoid.html

A Monoid adds a third:

- *Identity:* There's a neutral element e such that a ⊕ e = a.

Conceptually, Monoid extends Semigroup, but in Elixir, protocols must be defined independently.

Some types have a well-understood way to combine. Lists, for example, use concatenation as their canonical monoid.

Other types can be combined in multiple valid ways. Numbers might be combined by addition, multiplication, maximum, or minimum, so the number alone doesn't tell us which monoid we mean.

Since we can't infer the monoid from the value alone, we need a way to make the combination strategy explicit. In Elixir, we can use a struct.

As with many functional programming concepts, the underlying ideas are consistent, but the names vary across languages and libraries. The identity element might be called identity, start, or zero, while the combination function could appear as append, concat, combine, or add.

For consistency, we'll continue to follow Haskell's naming. Haskell uses mempty and mappend, so we'll adopt Monoid.empty and Monoid.append.

## Define the Protocol

First, let's define our protocol:

A Monoid must define empty/1 and append/2.

```
lib/fun_park/monoid.ex
defprotocol FunPark.Monoid do
  def empty(monoid_struct)
  def append(monoid_struct_a, monoid_struct_b)
  def wrap(monoid_struct, value)
  def unwrap(monoid_struct)
end
```

A Monoid must define two operations:

- empty/1: Returns the identity element. When combined with any value, it leaves that value unchanged—like adding zero in the context of Sum.
- append/2: Combines two values in an associative way, meaning the grouping doesn't affect the result—(a ⊕ b) ⊕ c is the same as a ⊕ (b ⊕ c).

Our protocol also includes wrap/2 and unwrap/1. These aren't part of the monoid laws, but since our combination logic lives inside the struct, we include them to provide a consistent way to lift and extract raw values.

# Combine Numbers with Sum

Our Ride expert notes that our more modern rides have their wait times generated from multiple sensors, so we need to be able to add these values together.

Combining numbers in the context of addition is the job for the Sum Monoid.

The Monoid.Sum module defines a struct initialized with 0, which serves as the identity for addition—when combined, it leaves the other number unchanged.

lib/fun_park/monoid/sum.ex
```elixir
defmodule FunPark.Monoid.Sum do
  defstruct value: 0
end
```

Next, we implement the Monoid protocol for Sum:

lib/fun_park/monoid/sum.ex
```elixir
defimpl FunPark.Monoid, for: FunPark.Monoid.Sum do
  alias FunPark.Monoid.Sum

  def empty(_), do: %Sum{}

  def append(%Sum{value: a}, %Sum{value: b}) do
    %Sum{value: a + b}
  end

  def wrap(%Sum{}, value) when is_number(value), do: %Sum{value: value}

  def unwrap(%Sum{value: value}) when is_number(value), do: value
end
```

- empty/1: Returns the identity—an empty Sum struct with a value of 0.
- append/2: Adds the values inside two Sum structs.
- wrap/2: Lifts a number into the monoid struct.
- unwrap/1: Extracts the number from the monoid struct.

## Run It

Start Elixir's iex shell and run mix to compile the code and load the project.

```
iex -S mix
```

Elixir allows us to manually create wrapped values:

```elixir
iex> sum_1 = %FunPark.Monoid.Sum{value: 1}
%FunPark.Monoid.Sum{value: 1}

iex> sum_2 = %FunPark.Monoid.Sum{value: 2}
%FunPark.Monoid.Sum{value: 2}
```

However, as a general rule, we avoid constructing structs directly. It's better to decouple by using Monoid.wrap/2, which lifts a raw value into the monoid context without exposing internal details:

```
iex> sum_1 = FunPark.Monoid.wrap(%FunPark.Monoid.Sum{}, 1)
%FunPark.Monoid.Sum{value: 1}

iex> sum_2 = FunPark.Monoid.wrap(%FunPark.Monoid.Sum{}, 2)
%FunPark.Monoid.Sum{value: 2}
```

Then we can use append/2 to combine the values within the context of Monoid.Sum:

```
iex> value = FunPark.Monoid.append(sum_1, sum_2)
%FunPark.Monoid.Sum{value: 3}
```

And we unwrap the final value:

```
iex> FunPark.Monoid.unwrap(value)
3
```

### Joe asks:
### All This Just to Add Two Numbers?

It might feel like overkill, but the goal is to build the mental model. Once you're fluent with monoids, you'll be able to apply the same pattern to more complex problems.

## Appendable

The caller shouldn't need to worry about all the wrapping and unwrapping—that's an internal concern. Let's define m_append/3 as a higher-level helper and handle the machinery behind the scenes. The m_ prefix, borrowed from Haskell's mappend, signals that this is a monoid-aware function.

lib/fun_park/monoid/utils.ex
```
def m_append(monoid, a, b) when is_struct(monoid) do
  append(wrap(monoid, a), wrap(monoid, b)) |> unwrap()
end
```

Notice that m_append/3 doesn't use empty/1. Combining two values doesn't require an identity element.

## Run It

In the context of Monoid.Sum, combine 1 and 2:

```
iex> FunPark.Monoid.Utils.m_append(%FunPark.Monoid.Sum{}, 1, 2)
3
```

We get 3, blissfully unaware of the internal wrapping logic.

We can combine a list of values by recursively applying append/2, starting from the monoid's identity. But another option exists: we can fold the list.

## Foldable

For a list, folding requires three components: the structure to reduce, a function to combine its contents, and a base case. A Monoid provides: append/2 for combination and empty/1 for the identity.

Since folding can proceed from left to right or right to left, our Foldable protocol supports both directions:

```
lib/fun_park/foldable.ex
defprotocol FunPark.Foldable do
  def fold_l(structure, transform_fn, base)
  def fold_r(structure, transform_fn, base)
end
```

With this, we can implement fold for lists:

```
lib/fun_park/list.ex
defimpl FunPark.Foldable, for: List do
  def fold_l(list, acc, func), do: :lists.foldl(func, acc, list)

  def fold_r(list, acc, func), do: :lists.foldr(func, acc, list)
end
```

Here we're using Erlang's :lists.foldl/3 and :lists.foldr/3 but adapting them to Elixir conventions: snake_case names and data-first argument order.

We can fold a list using the rules of a monoid. In Haskell, this pattern is called mconcat; we'll call ours m_concat/2.

```
lib/fun_park/monoid/utils.ex
def m_concat(monoid, values) when is_struct(monoid) and is_list(values) do
  fold_l(values, empty(monoid), fn value, acc ->
    append(acc, wrap(monoid, value))
  end)
  |> unwrap()
end
```

This starts with the monoid's identity value and iterates through the list, applying append/2 to combine each item with the accumulated result. Finally, unwrap/1 extracts and returns the combined value. With m_concat/2, we've generalized list reduction with a monoid.

## Math

Monoids are typically abstracted from the caller with a function that hides the details. We can take Monoid.Sum one step further by wrapping it in a Math module. After all, the caller doesn't care that a monoid is doing the work—they just want a total.

lib/fun_park/math.ex
```elixir
def sum(a, b) do
  m_append(%Monoid.Sum{}, a, b)
end

def sum(list) when is_list(list) do
  m_concat(%Monoid.Sum{}, list)
end
```

## Run It

Now we can add two Ride wait time sensors:

```
iex> FunPark.Math.sum(1, 2)
3
```

And we can add a collection of sensors:

```
iex> FunPark.Math.sum([1, 2, 3])
6
```

Or we can even add a single sensor:

```
iex> FunPark.Math.sum([3])
3
```

And when there are no sensors at all, the monoid still knows what to do:

```
iex> FunPark.Math.sum([])
0
```

Our Ride expert just wanted to add wait times. Building an entire monoid might seem like overkill—especially since Elixir already provides Enum.sum/1.

But now we have something Elixir doesn't: a generic, composable monoidal system.

And a monoid isn't limited to combining concrete values—it can also combine abstract behavior. An Eq monoid, for instance, merges equality relations rather than data, allowing us to define complex equivalence conditions by combining simple ones.

> I have a soft spot for monoids—they were the first time I realized functional programming wasn't just about constructing pipelines to transform values but also about composing *concepts*: rules, behaviors, and strategies. They're not just a way to structure code but a way to structure thought.

# Combine Equality

You can combine equality in two ways:

- All: Every equality check must return true.
- Any: At least one equality check must return true.

Before we tackle implementation, we need to address *bias*, a structural preference for one outcome over another. In the Monoid context, All is biased toward true: it starts from true and flips to false if any condition fails. Any, by contrast, is biased toward false: it starts from false and flips to true as soon as one condition passes.

## Equal All

Our FastPass expert notes that the system occasionally produces duplicate passes as a side effect of syncing data across multiple services and queues under high load. To manage this, we need to identify when two FastPasses are effectively duplicates—specifically, when they share the same ride and time.

The straightforward solution is to write a one-off that applies both eq?/2 checks and returns true if both succeed. But hardcoding logic like this tends to sprawl—making it harder to reuse, reason about, or update later. Instead, let's generalize the solution for any case where multiple equality checks need to be combined in a conjunctive context.

### Construct the Monoid

First, we define the struct, including the identity for Eq.All, which is true. Equality is assumed to hold unless a comparison shows otherwise. (The code is on the next page.)

lib/fun_park/monoid/eq_all.ex
```elixir
defmodule FunPark.Monoid.Eq.All do
  defstruct eq?: &FunPark.Monoid.Eq.All.default_eq?/2,
            not_eq?: &FunPark.Monoid.Eq.All.default_not_eq?/2

  def default_eq?(_, _), do: true
  def default_not_eq?(_, _), do: false
end
```

Next, we implement the monoid:

lib/fun_park/monoid/eq_all.ex
```elixir
defimpl FunPark.Monoid, for: FunPark.Monoid.Eq.All do
  alias FunPark.Eq.Utils
  alias FunPark.Monoid.Eq.All

  def empty(_), do: %All{}

  def append(%All{} = eq1, %All{} = eq2) do
    %All{
      eq?: fn a, b -> eq1.eq?.(a, b) && eq2.eq?.(a, b) end,
      not_eq?: fn a, b -> eq1.not_eq?.(a, b) || eq2.not_eq?.(a, b) end
    }
  end

  def wrap(%All{}, eq) do
    eq = Utils.to_eq_map(eq)
    %All{
      eq?: eq.eq?,
      not_eq?: eq.not_eq?
    }
  end

  def unwrap(%All{eq?: eq?, not_eq?: not_eq?}) do
    %{eq?: eq?, not_eq?: not_eq?}
  end
end
```

The append logic uses &&, so two values are considered equal only if *all* equality checks agree. If any single check returns false, the comparison short-circuits and fails. The not_eq?/2 function is its logical inverse—it returns true if *any* individual check reports inequality.

Like Math.sum, we can abstract away the monoid inside Eq.Utils:

lib/fun_park/eq/utils.ex
```elixir
def append_all(a, b) do
  m_append(%Monoid.Eq.All{}, a, b)
end

def concat_all(eq_list) when is_list(eq_list) do
  m_concat(%Monoid.Eq.All{}, eq_list)
end
```

Eq.All handles the combination of multiple equality checks behind the scenes, without exposing the monoid.

## Run It

First, create two different FastPasses that share the same ride and time:

```
iex> datetime = DateTime.new!(~D[2025-06-01], ~T[13:00:00])
iex> apple = FunPark.Ride.make("Apple Cart")
iex> fast_pass_a = FunPark.FastPass.make(apple, datetime)
iex> fast_pass_b = FunPark.FastPass.make(apple, datetime)
```

Next, retrieve the existing eq_ride/0 and eq_time/0 comparators and combine them using concat_all/1:

```
iex> eq_ride = FunPark.FastPass.eq_ride()
iex> eq_time = FunPark.FastPass.eq_time()
iex> eq_both = FunPark.Eq.Utils.concat_all([eq_ride, eq_time])
```

From the perspective of the FastPass context, these passes are different—they have unique IDs. But since they match in both ride and time, eq_ride/0, eq_time/0, and eq_both/0 all return true:

```
iex> FunPark.Eq.Utils.eq?(fast_pass_a, fast_pass_b)
false
iex> FunPark.Eq.Utils.eq?(fast_pass_a, fast_pass_b, eq_ride)
true
iex> FunPark.Eq.Utils.eq?(fast_pass_a, fast_pass_b, eq_time)
true
iex> FunPark.Eq.Utils.eq?(fast_pass_a, fast_pass_b, eq_both)
true
```

Let's say the time on fast_pass_a is updated:

```
iex> datetime_2 = DateTime.new!(~D[2025-06-01], ~T[14:00:00])
iex> fast_pass_a = FunPark.FastPass.change(fast_pass_a, %{time: datetime_2})
```

eq_ride/0 still returns true, but eq_time/0 and eq_both/0 now return false:

```
iex> FunPark.Eq.Utils.eq?(fast_pass_a, fast_pass_b, eq_ride)
true
iex> FunPark.Eq.Utils.eq?(fast_pass_a, fast_pass_b, eq_time)
false
iex> FunPark.Eq.Utils.eq?(fast_pass_a, fast_pass_b, eq_both)
false
```

### Add to FastPass

We can implement this logic in the FastPass bounded context.

lib/fun_park/fast_pass.ex
```
def eq_ride_and_time do
  Eq.Utils.concat_all([eq_ride(), eq_time()])
end
```

This defines a new equality by name and time, not as a one-off but by composing existing rules.

## Equal Any

But wait—we didn't quite get this right. Our FastPass expert notes that we don't just want to identify passes that are equal by ride and time. We also want to treat passes with the same id as equal, even if their internal details are different.

To manage this, we need to determine when two FastPasses match by id *or* by ride and time—a case of disjunctive equality, where satisfying any rule is sufficient.

### Construct the Monoid

We begin by defining the struct, with the identity for Eq.Any set to false. Values are considered not equal unless explicitly defined otherwise.

lib/fun_park/monoid/eq_any.ex
```
defmodule FunPark.Monoid.Eq.Any do
  defstruct eq?: &FunPark.Monoid.Eq.Any.default_eq?/2,
            not_eq?: &FunPark.Monoid.Eq.Any.default_not_eq?/2

  def default_eq?(_, _), do: false

  def default_not_eq?(_, _), do: true
end
```

Then we implement the Monoid protocol:

lib/fun_park/monoid/eq_any.ex
```
defimpl FunPark.Monoid, for: FunPark.Monoid.Eq.Any do
  alias FunPark.Eq.Utils
  alias FunPark.Monoid.Eq.Any

  def empty(_), do: %Any{}

  def append(%Any{} = eq1, %Any{} = eq2) do
    %Any{
      eq?: fn a, b -> eq1.eq?.(a, b) || eq2.eq?.(a, b) end,
      not_eq?: fn a, b -> eq1.not_eq?.(a, b) && eq2.not_eq?.(a, b) end
    }
  end
end
```

```
  def wrap(%Any{}, eq) do
    eq = Utils.to_eq_map(eq)

    %Any{
      eq?: eq.eq?,
      not_eq?: eq.not_eq?
    }
  end

  def unwrap(%Any{eq?: eq?, not_eq?: not_eq?}) do
    %{eq?: eq?, not_eq?: not_eq?}
  end
end
```

The append logic uses ||, so two values are considered equal if any combined equality check returns true. It short-circuits on the first successful match.

The not_eq?/2 function is its logical inverse: it returns true only if *all* checks return false, meaning none of the equality rules matched.

Like Eq.All, we abstract away the monoid details in Eq.Utils:

lib/fun_park/eq/utils.ex
```
def append_any(a, b) do
  m_append(%Monoid.Eq.Any{}, a, b)
end
```

lib/fun_park/eq/utils.ex
```
def concat_any(eq_list) when is_list(eq_list) do
  m_concat(%Monoid.Eq.Any{}, eq_list)
end
```

Now we can express our FastPass expert's duplication logic by combining the default equality with our earlier eq_ride_and_time/0. A pair of passes is considered duplicates if *either* condition is satisfied.

lib/fun_park/fast_pass.ex
```
def duplicate_pass do
  Eq.Utils.concat_any([Eq, eq_ride_and_time()])
end
```

Our duplicate_pass/0 function is declarative: it describes *what* makes two passes duplicates and leaves the monoids to handle *how* the comparison is performed.

**Run It**

First, let's generate a couple of FastPasses:

```
iex> datetime = DateTime.new!(~D[2025-06-01], ~T[13:00:00])
iex> tea_cup = FunPark.Ride.make("Tea Cup")

iex> pass_a = FunPark.FastPass.make(tea_cup, datetime)
iex> pass_b = FunPark.FastPass.make(tea_cup, datetime)
```

These have different IDs, so the default Eq determines they are not equal:

```
iex> FunPark.Eq.Utils.eq?(pass_a, pass_b)
false
```

But from the perspective of our duplicate check, they are considered the same:

```
iex> dup_pass_check = FunPark.FastPass.duplicate_pass()
iex> FunPark.Eq.Utils.eq?(pass_a, pass_b, dup_pass_check)
true
```

Let's update the first pass to point to a different ride:

```
iex> mansion = FunPark.Ride.make("Haunted Mansion")
iex> pass_a_changed = FunPark.FastPass.change(pass_a, %{ride: mansion})
```

The updated pass still matches the original because the ID hasn't changed:

```
iex> FunPark.Eq.Utils.eq?(pass_a, pass_a_changed, dup_pass_check)
true
```

But the duplicate check no longer considers pass_b to be equal, as they have different IDs and rides:

```
iex> FunPark.Eq.Utils.eq?(pass_b, pass_a_changed, dup_pass_check)
false
```

By composing simple equality rules with a monoid, we've captured the domain's definition of duplication—making logic easier to express, reuse, and adapt as our understanding deepens.

# Combine Order

Our Patron expert mentions that patrons have a defined priority: first by ticket tier, then by reward points. To support this, we need to combine our Ord logic.

The Sum monoid—and even the Eq monoids—might feel like overkill, since one-off implementations are easy to write. But combining Ord is genuinely hard, which is why many codebases end up with inefficient sorts.

The key insight is that this isn't a sorting problem—it's a combination problem. A monoid lets us solve the hard part once and reuse it wherever needed.

## Construct the Monoid

When creating any Monoid, the first step is identifying the *identity*—a value that, when combined with others, leaves them unchanged.

For Ord, the identity is a *no-op*: all comparisons return false. The bias for Ord is *incomparable*: elements are assumed unordered unless a rule defines their relationship.

lib/fun_park/monoid/ord.ex
```
defmodule FunPark.Monoid.Ord do
  defstruct lt?: &FunPark.Monoid.Ord.default?/2,
            le?: &FunPark.Monoid.Ord.default?/2,
            gt?: &FunPark.Monoid.Ord.default?/2,
            ge?: &FunPark.Monoid.Ord.default?/2

  def default?(_, _), do: false
end
```

Next, we implement the Monoid protocol. Like the Sum and Eq monoids, Ord has a single known identity, so empty/1 returns the default struct.

lib/fun_park/monoid/ord.ex
```
def empty(_) do
  %Ord{}
end
```

Our append/2 function is concise, making it a bit hard to read:

lib/fun_park/monoid/ord.ex
```
def append(%Ord{} = ord1, %Ord{} = ord2) do
  %Ord{
    lt?: fn a, b ->
      cond do
        ord1.lt?.(a, b) -> true
        ord1.gt?.(a, b) -> false
        true -> ord2.lt?.(a, b)
      end
    end,
    le?: fn a, b ->
      cond do
        ord1.lt?.(a, b) -> true
        ord1.gt?.(a, b) -> false
        true -> ord2.le?.(a, b)
```

```
      end
    end,
    gt?: fn a, b ->
      cond do
        ord1.gt?.(a, b) -> true
        ord1.lt?.(a, b) -> false
        true -> ord2.gt?.(a, b)
      end
    end,
    ge?: fn a, b ->
      cond do
        ord1.gt?.(a, b) -> true
        ord1.lt?.(a, b) -> false
        true -> ord2.ge?.(a, b)
      end
    end
  }
end
```

## Breaking Down lt?/2

Let's take a closer look at lt?/2:

1. Ask the first Ord (ord1) whether a < b. If it returns true, the result is true.
2. If ord1 says a > b, return false.
3. If neither is true, treat a and b as equal under ord1 and delegate the decision to ord2.

This creates a *lexicographic ordering*: each Ord is applied in sequence and only contributes if the previous one considers the elements equal. The first Ord to distinguish the elements determines the result.

Finally, we need our wrap logic:

lib/fun_park/monoid/ord.ex
```
def wrap(%Ord{}, ord) do
  ord = Utils.to_ord_map(ord)

  %Ord{
    lt?: ord.lt?,
    le?: ord.le?,
    gt?: ord.gt?,
    ge?: ord.ge?
  }
end

def unwrap(%Ord{lt?: lt?, le?: le?, gt?: gt?, ge?: ge?}) do
  %{
    lt?: lt?,
    le?: le?,
    gt?: gt?,
```

```
    ge?: ge?
  }
end
```

### Abstract the Monoid

Callers don't need to know that this composition is powered by a monoid, so we'll abstract it in Ord.Utils:

lib/fun_park/ord/utils.ex
```
def append(a, b) do
  m_append(%FunPark.Monoid.Ord{}, a, b)
end
```

lib/fun_park/ord/utils.ex
```
def concat(ord_list) when is_list(ord_list) do
  m_concat(%FunPark.Monoid.Ord{}, ord_list)
end
```

## Run It

First, let's create the patrons Alice, Beth, and Charles:

```
iex> alice = FunPark.Patron.make(
    "Alice", 15, 50, reward_points: 50, ticket_tier: :premium
    )
iex> beth = FunPark.Patron.make(
    "Beth", 16, 55, reward_points: 20, ticket_tier: :vip
    )
iex> charles = FunPark.Patron.make(
    "Charles", 14, 60, reward_points: 50, ticket_tier: :premium
    )
```

The default sort for Patrons is alphabetical by name, resulting in Alice, Beth, and then Charles:

```
iex> FunPark.List.sort([charles, beth, alice])
[
  %FunPark.Patron{
    name: "Alice",
    ticket_tier: :premium,
    reward_points: 50,
    ...
  },
  %FunPark.Patron{
    name: "Beth",
    ticket_tier: :vip,
    reward_points: 20,
    ...
  },
  %FunPark.Patron{
```

```
    name: "Charles",
    ticket_tier: :premium,
    reward_points: 50,
    ...
  }
]
```

The priority sort combines ord_by_ticket_tier/0 and ord_by_reward_points/0:

```
iex> ord_ticket = FunPark.Patron.ord_by_ticket_tier()
iex> ord_reward_points = FunPark.Patron.ord_by_reward_points()
iex> ord_priority = FunPark.Ord.Utils.concat([ord_ticket, ord_reward_points])
iex> FunPark.List.sort([charles, beth, alice], ord_priority)
[
  %FunPark.Patron{
    name: "Charles",
    ticket_tier: :premium,
    reward_points: 50,
    ...
  },
  %FunPark.Patron{
    name: "Alice",
    ticket_tier: :premium,
    reward_points: 50,
    ...
  },
  %FunPark.Patron{
    name: "Beth",
    ticket_tier: :vip,
    reward_points: 20,
    ...
  }
]
```

Beth is greater than Alice and Charles due to her VIP status. However, our Patron expert notes that this isn't quite right—patrons with the same priority should still be sorted by name.

```
iex> ord_priority = FunPark.Ord.Utils.concat(
    [ord_ticket, ord_reward_points, FunPark.Ord]
)
iex> FunPark.List.sort([charles, beth, alice], ord_priority)
[
  %FunPark.Patron{
    name: "Alice",
    ticket_tier: :premium,
    reward_points: 50,
    ...
  },
```

```
%FunPark.Patron{
  name: "Charles",
  ticket_tier: :premium,
  reward_points: 50,
  ...
},
%FunPark.Patron{
  name: "Beth",
  ticket_tier: :vip,
  reward_points: 20,
  ...
}
]
```

Now the sorting is correct: Beth remains the highest due to her VIP status, while Alice and Charles, who share the same priority, are sorted alphabetically by name. More importantly, this entire sorting process happens in a single pass.

We can encapsulate this logic in our Patron module:

lib/fun_park/patron.ex
```
def ord_by_priority do
  Ord.Utils.concat([
    ord_by_ticket_tier(),
    ord_by_reward_points(),
    Ord
  ])
end
```

We leveraged the monoid to solve the problem and then abstracted it away. What was once difficult and error-prone is now simple, readable, and reusable.

# Generalize Maximum

Our Ride expert needs a daily report from each ride's wait time log. They want the maximum wait time recorded that day, a single number that reflects the peak demand for the ride.

Sometimes we don't care about full ordering—we just need the highest value. Max is a monoid that uses an Ord instance to extract the largest result.

### Construct the Monoid

The Monoid.Max struct encapsulates both the value and the ordering logic:

lib/fun_park/monoid/max.ex
```
defmodule FunPark.Monoid.Max do
  defstruct value: nil, ord: FunPark.Ord
end
```

Like all monoids, Max requires an identity element. However, unlike Sum or Ord, we cannot assume a default. Instead, the caller needs to specify the appropriate value with empty/1:

lib/fun_park/monoid/max.ex
```
def empty(%Max{value: min_value, ord: ord}) do
  %Max{value: min_value, ord: ord}
end
```

In the Ord chapter, you created a max/3 function, which should look something like this:

lib/fun_park/ord/utils.ex
```
def max(a, b, ord \\ Ord) do
  case compare(a, b, ord) do
    :lt -> b
    _ -> a
  end
end
```

We can leverage that max/3 for the Monoid's append/2:

lib/fun_park/monoid/max.ex
```
def append(%Max{value: a, ord: ord}, %Max{value: b}) do
  %Max{value: Utils.max(a, b, ord), ord: ord}
end
```

And finally, we provide the wrap/2 and unwrap/1 functions:

lib/fun_park/monoid/max.ex
```
def wrap(%Max{ord: ord}, value) do
  %Max{value: value, ord: Utils.to_ord_map(ord)}
end

def unwrap(%Max{value: value}), do: value
```

### Abstract the Monoid

Callers don't need to know that max/2 is powered by a monoid, so we abstract it in the Math module:

lib/fun_park/math.ex
```
def max(a, b) do
  m_append(%Monoid.Max{value: Float.min_finite()}, a, b)
end

def max(list) when is_list(list) do
  m_concat(%Monoid.Max{value: Float.min_finite()}, list)
end
```

The preceding code operates in the domain of numbers, so for Max we use Float.min_finite(), which acts as a *sentinel value*—a value that stands in for a concept. In this monoid, any real number will replace the sentinel during comparison.

## Run It

We can use max/2 to find the larger of two numbers:

```
iex> FunPark.Math.max(1, 2)
2
```

And max/1 solves our Ride expert's daily report from a ride's wait time log:

```
iex> log = [20, 30, 10, 20, 15, 10, 20]
iex> FunPark.Math.max(log)
30
```

Like all Monoids, Max also works with a single value:

```
iex> FunPark.Math.max([3])
3
```

And for an empty list, it returns the identity—in this case, Elixir's smallest possible number:

```
iex> FunPark.Math.max([])
-1.7976931348623157e308
```

## What About Elixir's Built-In max?

Elixir's max/2 returns the larger of two numbers and behaves like a semi-group—it can combine two values, but it lacks an identity for handling empty or single-element cases. max has no built-in monoid, and no generic Max works across custom types. So if we want a composable Max that integrates with domain-specific ordering, we have to define it ourselves.

## Prioritize a Patron

Our Patron expert informs us that we don't just need a priority sort; we need a true priority queue: logic to retrieve the next, highest-priority patron.

As with any monoid, we begin with an identity—here, a value representing the lowest possible priority. Let's use a synthetic Patron as a sentinel, with reward_points set to the smallest finite float and ticket_tier set to nil, ensuring that any real patron always takes precedence.

lib/fun_park/patron.ex
```
def priority_empty do
  %__MODULE__{reward_points: Float.min_finite(), ticket_tier: nil}
end
```

To create a Max monoid instance, we supply it with our priority_empty/0 and ord_by_priority/0 logic:

lib/fun_park/patron.ex
```
defp max_priority_monoid do
  %Monoid.Max{
    value: priority_empty(),
    ord: ord_by_priority()
  }
end
```

## Abstract the Monoid

Again, callers don't need to know that highest_priority/1 is powered by a monoid, so we can further abstract that detail.

lib/fun_park/patron.ex
```
def highest_priority(patrons) when is_list(patrons) do
  m_concat(max_priority_monoid(), patrons)
end
```

The highest_priority/1 function folds a list of patrons, returning the one with the highest priority.

- Ord defines how to compare patrons—first by ticket tier, then by reward points.
- Max uses that comparison to keep the greater of two patrons.
- The Monoid protocol provides a consistent interface for combining values.
- m_concat/2 performs the reduction.
- highest_priority/1 abstracts all these internal details from the caller.

> This is the essence of functional composition: breaking down behavior into small, focused parts and building complex results by composing them. That's how mastery builds—not by memorizing solutions but by assembling deeper models that let us reason more effectively.

## Run It

Beth has more reward points than Alice, so she has a higher priority and will be selected first:

```
iex> alice = FunPark.Patron.make("Alice", 15, 150)
iex> beth = FunPark.Patron.make("Beth", 15, 150, reward_points: 100)

iex> FunPark.Patron.highest_priority([beth, alice])
%FunPark.Patron{
  name: "Beth",
  ticket_tier: :basic,
  reward_points: 100,
  ...
}
```

If Alice upgrades her ticket to VIP, she gains a higher priority than Beth, since ticket tier takes precedence over reward points:

```
iex> alice = FunPark.Patron.change(alice, %{ticket_tier: :vip})

iex> FunPark.Patron.highest_priority([beth, alice])
%FunPark.Patron{
  name: "Alice",
  ticket_tier: :vip,
  reward_points: 0,
  ...
}
```

The Max monoid also works when there's only a single patron in the list:

```
iex> FunPark.Patron.highest_priority([beth])
%FunPark.Patron{
  name: "Beth",
  ticket_tier: :basic,
  reward_points: 100,
  ...
}
```

If there are no patrons, the sentinel value is returned:

```
iex(10)> FunPark.Patron.highest_priority([])
%FunPark.Patron{
  id: nil,
  name: nil,
  ticket_tier: nil,
  reward_points: -1.7976931348623157e308,
  ...
}
```

By its nature a priority queue can be empty, and we represent this state using a sentinel, requiring the caller to recognize that the placeholder does not represent a real patron. In the upcoming Maybe chapter, Model Absence in a Monoid, on page 129, we'll explore better techniques for handling situations like this.

### Act on It

Try building a couple of new monoids on your own:

- Product: Combines numbers through multiplication.
- Min: Selects the smallest value using an Ord instance.

Follow the same pattern you saw in Sum and Max: implement empty/1, append/2, wrap/2, and unwrap/1. The goal is to get comfortable applying the Monoid structure in different contexts.

Find the Monoid Chapter Answers, on page 212.

## Manage Complexity

Software complexity can be measured in many ways, each offering insight into how difficult a function or system is to understand, modify, and extend. For now, let's focus on *cyclomatic complexity*, which measures the number of independent paths through a function, reflecting how difficult it is to test and modify.

- A score of 1–4 indicates simple logic that is easy to understand and maintain.
- A score of 5–10 suggests moderate complexity, where changes require careful consideration.
- A score above 10 signals high complexity, making the function difficult to extend and maintain.

Let's revisit sorting our patrons by priority and see how our declarative approach manages cyclomatic complexity.

### The Hidden Cost of Imperative Code

Patrons have a ticket tier, reward points, and a name, and we need to sort them. Here is an imperative approach:

```
def ord_by_priority(patrons) do
  Enum.sort(patrons, fn a, b ->
    cond do
      a.ticket_tier == :vip and b.ticket_tier != :vip ->
        true
```

```
      b.ticket_tier == :vip and a.ticket_tier != :vip ->
        false

      a.ticket_tier == :premium and b.ticket_tier not in [:vip, :premium] ->
        true

      b.ticket_tier == :premium and a.ticket_tier not in [:vip, :premium] ->
        false

      a.reward_points < b.reward_points ->
        true

      a.reward_points > b.reward_points ->
        false

      a.name > b.name ->
        true

      a.name < b.name ->
        false

      true ->
        false
    end
  end)
end
```

This style is common in teams focused on closing tickets quickly. It's a direct set of instructions: do this, then that. The goal is to implement a rule, not to shape the system.

Count the decision points and you'll find nine, giving this function a cyclomatic complexity of nine.

What happens when our Patron expert introduces a new business rule, such as patrons with 50 or more reward points receiving the same priority as those with a ticket upgrade?

Where do you start?

## More What You'd Call "Guidelines" Than Actual Rules

You didn't write the original sorting logic, so first, you need to untangle its nine decision points, the upper limit of what you can reasonably hold in short-term memory. What is this code actually doing, and where is it applied? After tracing the logic, you implement the new priority rule.

Then a bug is reported. You missed a subtle reversal, and your change broke the sort.

You fix it—only to discover the function was copied elsewhere, with a slightly different variation. You track them down and apply the same fix.

Then another issue: one of those components relied on the old behavior. You revert that version.

Later, the expert clarifies the rule: the priority boost should only apply to upgrades from Basic to Premium, not VIP. Another developer takes that ticket, repeats the same process, and introduces a fresh set of inconsistencies.

Each round adds friction. The logic grows harder to follow. Bugs multiply. And the real problem remains: the rules are simple, the code is not.

This cycle continues, with every new requirement adding more variation and more chances for mistakes. The problem isn't the domain—it's the code. As *Out of the Tar Pit* puts it, "the majority of complexity is accidental," introduced not by the problem we're solving but by how we chose to solve it.[2] Without clear models to reason from, understanding becomes local, brittle, and hard to share. Each developer has to rediscover the same fragile paths through the logic.

As the codebase locks up, deadlines slip and features stall, so more developers are added.

But understanding doesn't parallelize, and complexity doesn't distribute. Each new contributor must climb the same tangled mess—only now, even more time is spent coordinating, clarifying, and patching over mismatches in mental models.

This is *Brooks' law [Bro95]* in action: adding people to a late project makes it later.

## Reduce Complexity with Declarative Logic

The imperative approach shows *how* a task is accomplished, laying out every step explicitly. Declarative code, in contrast, focuses on *what* should happen, abstracting details into composable building blocks. Here's an example of the ord_by_priority logic written declaratively.

```
def ord_by_priority do
  ord_by_ticket_tier()
  |> append(ord_by_reward_points())
  |> append(Ord)
end
```

---

2.  https://curtclifton.net/papers/MoseleyMarks06a.pdf

The ord_by_priority/0 function specifies the ordering: first by ticket tier, then by reward points, and finally by the patron's default, which is their name. This declarative code includes no branching logic, giving it a cyclomatic complexity of one—the lowest possible.

When our experts change their mind, deciding that patrons with higher ticket tiers and reward point scores should be listed first, it's just a matter of adding that bit of declarative logic to the pipeline.

```
def ord_by_priority do
  ord_by_ticket_tier()
  |> append(ord_by_reward_points())
  |> reverse()
  |> append(Ord)
end
```

Now ord_by_priority/0 orders by ticket tier and then by reward points, applies a reverse to prioritize higher values, and finally continues to fall back to the patron's default.

Declarative code resists the death spiral. Instead of unraveling dense control flow, we describe the intended behavior using composable rules. Each piece becomes a meaningful unit—a chunk we can understand and reuse. When requirements change, we refine those chunks rather than rebuilding everything from scratch.

That's not just cleaner code; it's a clearer mental model. Fewer branches means less to hold in working memory. We think in terms of structure and intention, not mechanical steps. And because the logic is declarative and consistent, it's easier for teams to understand, adapt, and extend together.

## What You've Learned

Eq and Ord gave us a way to define equality and ordering explicitly, turning vague comparisons into reusable rules.

With Monoid, we added structure to combination. Instead of hardcoding logic, we captured what it *means* to combine—whether it's summing numbers, merging lists, or resolving priorities.

These patterns—Eq, Ord, Monoid—aren't just abstractions. They're mental models. The more we use them, the more they shape how we see problems: as equality, ordering, or combination. And once we see the shape of a problem, we can reason about it more clearly and build solutions that scale.

So far, we've worked within a single bounded context. Next, we'll step beyond, where logic spans boundaries and composition becomes coordination.

> We all start by copying and pasting example code using our short-term memory. As we learn, we begin to move information into long-term memory, allowing us to organize and reshape what we know. That's where you want to be at this point in your journey—able to form new logic from the parts you've internalized.

# CHAPTER 5

# Define Logic with Predicates

A production-ready `Predicate` is available in the Funx library.[1]

Each chapter in this book introduces new mental models, and learning them takes effort.

This one adds several: treating predicates as composable structures, applying logic across domain boundaries, and composing functions whose shapes don't align.

The difficulty isn't just the concepts—it's also Elixir. While functional, Elixir has idioms that complicate composition: no built-in currying, a pipe operator that targets the first argument, and different syntax for named and anonymous functions—all reasonable choices, but they add friction.

You use predicates all the time: filtering a list, checking a condition, matching a pattern. Once you internalize the mental model—not just if statements but composable rules that follow Boolean logic—you can isolate decisions, avoid duplication, and build policies that stay flexible as they grow.

The *predicate* is a statement that can be true or false within a context. In code, it's a function that returns a Boolean—encapsulating a test that can be named, reused, and composed to express domain intent.

Because predicates follow Boolean algebra, they compose:

- *Conjunction (a ∧ b):* True if both are true.
- *Disjunction (a ∨ b):* True if at least one is true.
- *Negation (¬a):* Inverts the result.

---

1.  https://hexdocs.pm/funx/Funx.Predicate.html

These patterns scale. Complex policies, dynamic filters, validation pipelines—they all follow the same idea: combining small checks into larger ones.

## Simple Predicates

In the Ride context, our expert needs to determine whether a ride is currently online and whether it has a long wait time:

```
lib/fun_park/ride.ex
def online?(%__MODULE__{online: online}), do: online

def long_wait?(%__MODULE__{wait_time: wait_time}), do: wait_time > 30
```

### Run It

Start Elixir's iex shell and run the mix script to compile the code and load the project.

```
iex -S mix
```

Tired of typing? Don't forget the examples are available as Livebooks.[2]

Let's start by generating a Ride:

```
iex> tea_cup = FunPark.Ride.make("Tea Cup", online: true, wait_time: 100)
%FunPark.Ride{ name: "Tea Cup", wait_time: 100, online: true, ... }
```

The Tea Cup is online:

```
iex> FunPark.Ride.online?(tea_cup)
true
```

And it has a long wait:

```
iex> FunPark.Ride.long_wait?(tea_cup)
true
```

However, our expert also wants to check for a short wait, the opposite of a long wait. Defining short_wait?/1 as wait_time <= 30 might seem straightforward, but it introduces redundant logic. More importantly, it risks inconsistency—if a future developer updates long_wait?/1 without modifying short_wait?/1, the two checks will fall out of sync.

---

2.  https://www.funxlib.com/book-livebooks.html

To ensure consistency, short_wait?/1 should be defined as the logical inverse of long_wait?/1. We can implement negation with p_not/1, a higher-order function.

lib/fun_park/predicate.ex
```
def p_not(pred) when is_function(pred) do
  fn value -> not pred.(value) end
end
```

And we can define short_wait?/1 as the complement of long_wait?/1:

```
def short_wait?, do: p_not(&long_wait?/1)
```

These simple predicates give us clear, focused decisions we can compose—building more complex logic from small, reusable parts.

Our Ride expert has a new business rule: a ride is considered suggested if it is both online?/1 *and* has a short_wait?/1. To express this, we need to combine predicates.

## Combine Predicates

Predicate logic has well-defined rules for combination.

| Logic | Description |
|-------|-------------|
| and | Combines two predicates, returning true only if both return true. |
| or | Combines two predicates, returning true if at least one returns true. |
| all | Returns true only if every predicate in a set returns true. |
| any | Returns true if at least one predicate in a set returns true. |
| none | The inverse of any, returning true if none return true. |

We've already got the perfect tool for this—monoids! And the best part? Predicate composition only needs two: Predicate.All and Predicate.Any.

Conjunctive operations, like Predicate.All, are biased toward true: they assume all conditions will pass and flip to false as soon as one fails. Disjunctive operations, like Predicate.Any, are biased toward false: they assume failure and flip to true on the first condition that passes.

We'll see bias again in our Maybe and Either monads.

### All

The Predicate.All monoid combines predicates in the context of conjunction (∧), using an identity of () -> true. When we combined Eq, we combined state. With predicates, we're combining behavior, as shown on the next page.

lib/fun_park/monoid/pred_all.ex
```elixir
defmodule FunPark.Monoid.Predicate.All do
  defstruct value: &FunPark.Monoid.Predicate.All.default_pred?/1

  def default_pred?(_), do: true
end

defimpl FunPark.Monoid, for: FunPark.Monoid.Predicate.All do
  alias FunPark.Monoid.Predicate.All

  def empty(_), do: %All{}

  def append(%All{} = p1, %All{} = p2) do
    %All{
      value: fn value -> p1.value.(value) and p2.value.(value) end
    }
  end

  def wrap(%All{}, value) when is_function(value, 1) do
    %All{value: value}
  end

  def unwrap(%All{value: value}), do: value
end
```

## Any

The Predicate.Any monoid combines predicates in the context of disjunction (∨), using an identity of () -> false.

lib/fun_park/monoid/pred_any.ex
```elixir
defmodule FunPark.Monoid.Predicate.Any do
  defstruct value: &FunPark.Monoid.Predicate.Any.default_pred?/1

  def default_pred?(_), do: false
end

defimpl FunPark.Monoid, for: FunPark.Monoid.Predicate.Any do
  alias FunPark.Monoid.Predicate.Any

  def empty(_), do: %Any{}

  def append(%Any{} = p1, %Any{} = p2) do
    %Any{
      value: fn value -> p1.value.(value) or p2.value.(value) end
    }
  end

  def wrap(%Any{}, value) when is_function(value, 1) do
    %Any{value: value}
  end

  def unwrap(%Any{value: value}), do: value
end
```

> The best part about monoids is that they're closed under their operation—combine two, and you get another of the same kind. With predicates, every composition returns a predicate.

As in earlier chapters, let's abstract away the monoids and give callers higher-level operations instead:

lib/fun_park/predicate.ex
```elixir
defmodule FunPark.Predicate do
  import FunPark.Monoid.Utils, only: [m_append: 3, m_concat: 2]
  alias FunPark.Monoid.Predicate.{All, Any}

  def p_and(pred1, pred2) when is_function(pred1) and is_function(pred2) do
    m_append(%All{}, pred1, pred2)
  end

  def p_or(pred1, pred2) when is_function(pred1) and is_function(pred2) do
    m_append(%Any{}, pred1, pred2)
  end

  def p_not(pred) when is_function(pred) do
    fn value -> not pred.(value) end
  end

  def p_all(p_list) when is_list(p_list) do
    m_concat(%All{}, p_list)
  end

  def p_any(p_list) when is_list(p_list) do
    m_concat(%Any{}, p_list)
  end

  def p_none(p_list) when is_list(p_list) do
    p_not(p_any(p_list))
  end
end
```

We prefix these functions with p_, avoiding conflicts with Elixir's reserved words like and and or.

Now we can implement suggested?/1 by composing online?/1 with the negation of long_wait?/1, ensuring a ride is only suggested if it's available and the wait is short:

lib/fun_park/ride.ex
```elixir
def suggested?(%__MODULE__{} = ride),
  do: p_all([&online?/1, p_not(&long_wait?/1)]).(ride)
```

You'll find more than meets the eye in this simple function. Monoids can combine concrete values—like numbers using max or sum. But in this case, we're combining *ideas*. A predicate isn't a Boolean; it's a function that returns a Boolean.

> The suggested?/1 function is a wrapper—it takes a ride and immediately applies it to the predicate. In theory, we should be able to eliminate the wrapper with eta reduction. However, Elixir requires anonymous functions to be called explicitly with .() syntax. Because the outer function is named and the inner one is anonymous, we can't reduce it.

### Run It

The Tea Cup ride is not suggested because it has a wait time of 100 minutes:

```
iex> tea_cup = FunPark.Ride.make("Tea Cup", online: true, wait_time: 100)
%FunPark.Ride{ name: "Tea Cup", wait_time: 100, online: true, ...}

iex> FunPark.Ride.suggested?(tea_cup)
false
```

Later, the wait time for the Tea Cup ride shortens to 10 minutes, making it a suggested ride:

```
iex> tea_cup = FunPark.Ride.change(tea_cup, %{wait_time: 10})
%FunPark.Ride{ name: "Tea Cup", wait_time: 10, online: true, ... }

iex> FunPark.Ride.suggested?(tea_cup)
true
```

But our Ride expert is back—we're suggesting rides to patrons who aren't eligible! It won't do for patrons to follow our suggestion only to find out they can't take the ride.

So far, we've operated within a single bounded context. But with this request, our expert needs us to span both Ride and Patron.

## Predicates That Span Contexts

In *Domain-Driven Design [Eva03]*, when bounded contexts interact, their relationship is defined via *context mapping*. In FunPark, the Ride context sets eligibility rules—such as height and age requirements—while the Patron context supplies height and age attributes. This forms a *conformist relationship*, where Patron conforms to the rules set by Ride but has no influence over them.

Since the Ride defines the rules, the logic for determining eligibility belongs in the Ride bounded context.

To determine eligibility, a Ride must verify that a Patron meets height *and* age requirements.

First, let's define predicates for height and age requirements in the Ride context:

```
lib/fun_park/ride.ex
def tall_enough?(%Patron{} = patron, %__MODULE__{min_height: min_height}),
  do: Patron.get_height(patron) >= min_height
```

```
lib/fun_park/ride.ex
def old_enough?(%Patron{} = patron, %__MODULE__{min_age: min_age}),
  do: Patron.get_age(patron) >= min_age
```

Notice that we're not destructuring Patron to access age or height. How that data is stored is an implementation detail. The Ride context shouldn't rely on it—it should use Patron's accessors instead. This keeps the contexts loosely coupled and allows Patron to evolve without breaking Ride.

Next, we define eligible?/2 by combining the predicates using p_all/1:

```
def eligible?(%Patron{} = patron, %__MODULE__{} = ride),
  do: p_all([&tall_enough?/2, &old_enough?/2]).(patron, ride)
```

## Run It

Let's start with a patron and a ride:

```
iex> roller_mtn = FunPark.Ride.make(
  "Roller Mountain", min_height: 120, min_age: 12
)
%FunPark.Ride{ name: "Roller Mountain", min_age: 12, min_height: 120, ... }
iex> alice = FunPark.Patron.make("Alice", 13, 119)
%FunPark.Patron{ name: "Alice", age: 13, height: 119, ...}
```

Alice meets the age requirement but does not meet the height requirement:

```
iex> alice |> FunPark.Ride.old_enough?(roller_mtn)
true
iex> alice |> FunPark.Ride.tall_enough?(roller_mtn)
false
```

This means Alice is not eligible to ride Roller Mountain:

```
iex> alice |> FunPark.Ride.eligible?(roller_mtn)
false
```

However, if Alice grows a bit over the summer, she will be eligible:

```
iex> alice = FunPark.Patron.change(alice, %{height: 121})
%FunPark.Patron{ name: "Alice", age: 13, height: 121 }

iex> alice |> FunPark.Ride.eligible?(roller_mtn)
true
```

By composing logic across contexts, we're no longer suggesting rides a patron can't take.

We've enforced a rule across two contexts, without entangling them.

## Compose Multi-Arity Functions with Curry

Elixir is unusual among functional languages because it allows direct composition of functions with multiple arguments. In most functional languages, function composition is limited to *unary* functions—those that take a single argument.

For example, our eligible/2 function composes with the binary functions tall_enough?/2 and old_enough?/2. From a traditional functional programming perspective, this is odd:

```
def eligible?(%Patron{} = patron, %__MODULE__{} = ride),
  do: p_all([&tall_enough?/2, &old_enough?/2]).(patron, ride)
```

On one hand, this makes composing multi-argument functions straightforward. On the other, it raises a challenge: how do we compose functions with different arities?

Until now, all our predicates had the same shape. They slotted together easily. But real systems don't always cooperate, especially when logic spans across domains. Sometimes one function expects a Ride, while another needs both a Ride and a Patron.

So what happens when our Ride expert informs us that rides should only be suggested if patrons are also eligible? How do we combine suggested?/1, which belongs to the Ride context, with eligible?/2, which spans both Ride and Patron?

Fortunately, this isn't a new problem—it dates back over a hundred years to combinatory logic in lambda calculus. The solution, known as *curry* after Haskell Curry, transforms multi-argument functions into a sequence of unary functions by partially applying arguments one at a time.

Elixir doesn't have a built-in curry function, but we can define one. Early approaches—like the one described by Patrik Storm—use recursion and argument counting.[3] Our version takes a more direct approach:

lib/fun_park/utils.ex
```elixir
def curry(fun) when is_function(fun) do
  arity = :erlang.fun_info(fun, :arity) |> elem(1)
  curry(fun, arity, [])
end

defp curry(fun, 1, args),
  do: fn last_arg -> apply(fun, args ++ [last_arg]) end

defp curry(fun, arity, args) when arity > 1 do
  fn next_arg -> curry(fun, arity - 1, args ++ [next_arg]) end
end
```

The curry/1 function uses Erlang's fun_info/2 to retrieve the function's arity:

- If the function is already unary, it wraps it as-is.
- Otherwise, it applies arguments one at a time, recursively returning a new function until all arguments are provided.

Now we can add suggested?/2 to our Ride context, using curry/1 to partially apply eligible?/2, transforming it into eligible?/1. This allows us to compose it with suggested?/1, creating a predicate that suggests rides that are online, have short wait times, and where the patron is eligible to ride:

lib/fun_park/ride.ex
```elixir
def suggested?(%__MODULE__{} = ride),
  do: p_all([&online?/1, p_not(&long_wait?/1)]).(ride)

def suggested?(%Patron{} = patron, %__MODULE__{} = ride),
  do:
    p_all([
      &suggested?/1,
      curry(&eligible?/2).(patron)
    ]).(ride)
```

## Not So Fast

This is where the unary restriction becomes critical. We're not writing imperative code that calls a function, stores a value, and then applies it to another function. Instead, we're composing a single function that integrates all internal logic in one pass.

The issue is that while eligible?/2 has been transformed into eligible?/1, it still relies on tall_enough?/2 and old_enough?/2. This introduces a hidden problem: if

---

3.   http://blog.patrikstorm.com/function-currying-in-elixir

any function within the composition chain has a different arity, the entire chain breaks.

This is why languages like Haskell enforce unary functions. It may be less convenient, but it ensures that function composition remains consistent and predictable.

To prevent our predicates from breaking the chain, we need to curry all binary predicates before passing them to p_all/1:

lib/fun_park/ride.ex
```
def eligible?(%Patron{} = patron, %__MODULE__{} = ride),
  do:
    p_all([
      curry(&tall_enough?/2).(patron),
      curry(&old_enough?/2).(patron)
    ]).(ride)
```

lib/fun_park/ride.ex
```
def suggested?(%__MODULE__{} = ride),
  do: p_all([&online?/1, p_not(&long_wait?/1)]).(ride)

def suggested?(%Patron{} = patron, %__MODULE__{} = ride),
  do:
    p_all([
      &suggested?/1,
      curry(&eligible?/2).(patron)
    ]).(ride)
```

## Run It

Now we can check whether Roller Mountain is a suggested ride for Alice:

```
iex(14)> alice |> FunPark.Ride.suggested?(roller_mtn)
true
```

Yes, Alice meets both the height and age requirements, and the ride is currently online and without a long wait time.

If we take Roller Mountain offline, the result changes:

```
iex> roller_mtn = FunPark.Ride.change(roller_mtn, %{online: false})

iex> alice |> FunPark.Ride.suggested?(roller_mtn)
false
```

Since suggested?/1 requires a ride to be online, taking Roller Mountain offline prevents it from being a suggested ride.

# Harness Predicates for Collections

Unlike Eq or Ord, Elixir's Enum module integrates seamlessly with predicates—no extra logic or wrapping is needed.

| Function | Description |
|---|---|
| Enum.all?/2 | Returns true if all elements satisfy the predicate. |
| Enum.any?/2 | Returns true if at least one element satisfies the predicate. |
| Enum.count/2 | Counts elements that satisfy the predicate. |
| Enum.drop_while/2 | Drops elements from the beginning while the predicate returns true. |
| Enum.filter/2 | Returns a list of elements that satisfy the predicate. |
| Enum.find/2 | Returns the first element that satisfies the predicate. |
| Enum.find_index/2 | Returns the index of the first element that satisfies the predicate. |
| Enum.reject/2 | Returns a list of elements that do not satisfy the predicate. |
| Enum.take_while/2 | Takes elements from the beginning while the predicate returns true. |
| Enum.split_while/2 | Splits a list at the first element where the predicate returns false. |

## Run It

Let's start by defining a mixture of online and offline rides:

```
iex> thunder_loop = FunPark.Ride.make("Thunder Loop")
iex> ghost_hollow = FunPark.Ride.make("Ghost Hollow", online: false)
iex> rocket_ridge = FunPark.Ride.make("Rocket Ridge")
iex> jungle_river = FunPark.Ride.make("Jungle River", online: false)
iex> nebula_falls = FunPark.Ride.make("Nebula Falls")
iex> timber_twister = FunPark.Ride.make("Timber Twister", online: false)

iex> rides = [
  thunder_loop,
  ghost_hollow,
  rocket_ridge,
  jungle_river,
  nebula_falls,
  timber_twister
]
iex> online? = &FunPark.Ride.online?/1
```

Now we can use Enum functions to operate on this list.

## Predicate Checks

Availability rules in the `Ride` context often start with a simple question: Are all rides online? If not, are any available?

```
iex> rides |> Enum.all?(online?)
false

iex> rides |> Enum.any?(online?)
true
```

## Counting

To monitor availability, it helps to know how many rides are currently online; predicate-based counting makes this trivial.

```
iex> rides |> Enum.count(online?)
3
```

## Finding Elements

Sometimes it's useful to locate the first ride that's online—both the ride itself and its position in the list.

```
iex> rides |> Enum.find(online?)
%FunPark.Ride{name: "Thunder Loop", online: true, ...}

iex> rides |> Enum.find_index(online?)
0
```

## Filtering and Rejecting 'Elements

Sometimes we want a clean list of just the rides that are currently online.

```
iex> rides |> Enum.filter(online?)
[
  %FunPark.Ride{name: "Thunder Loop", online: true, ...},
  %FunPark.Ride{name: "Rocket Ridge", online: true, ...},
  %FunPark.Ride{name: "Nebula Falls", online: true, ...}
]
```

Or we want the opposite—a list of all rides that are currently not online:

```
iex> rides |> Enum.reject(online?)
[
  %FunPark.Ride{name: "Ghost Hollow", online: false, ...},
  %FunPark.Ride{name: "Jungle River", online: false, ...},
  %FunPark.Ride{name: "Timber Twister", online: false, ...}
]
```

## Taking and Dropping While

To reason about ride availability at the top of the list, we can isolate the initial online segment.

```
iex> rides |> Enum.take_while(online?)
[
  %FunPark.Ride{name: "Thunder Loop", online: true, ... },
]
```

We then examine everything that comes after, starting with the first offline ride.

```
iex> rides |> Enum.drop_while(online?)
[
  %FunPark.Ride{name: "Ghost Hollow", online: false, ...},
  %FunPark.Ride{ name: "Rocket Ridge", online: true, ...},
  %FunPark.Ride{name: "Jungle River", online: false, ...},
  %FunPark.Ride{name: "Nebula Falls", online: true, ...},
  %FunPark.Ride{name: "Timber Twister", online: false, ...}
]
```

## Splitting a List

Rather than taking or dropping, we can split the list at the first offline ride. This is useful for separating the initial run of available rides from the rest.

```
iex> rides |> Enum.split_while(online?)
{
  [
    %FunPark.Ride{name: "Thunder Loop", online: true, ...},
  ],
  [
    %FunPark.Ride{name: "Ghost Hollow", online: false, ...},
    %FunPark.Ride{name: "Rocket Ridge", online: true, ...}
    %FunPark.Ride{name: "Jungle River", online: false, ...},
    %FunPark.Ride{name: "Nebula Falls", online: true, ...},
    %FunPark.Ride{name: "Timber Twister", online: false, ...}
  ]
}
```

## Suggested Rides

Using Enum.filter/2, we can retrieve a list of suggested rides for a given patron:

lib/fun_park/ride.ex
```
def suggested_rides(%Patron{} = patron, rides) when is_list(rides) do
  Enum.filter(rides, &suggested?(patron, &1))
end
```

Rather than using curry to partially apply the suggested?/2 function, this uses Elixir's capture syntax, partially applying Patron and generating a unary function that takes Ride as its argument. Enum.filter/2 provides each ride as &1 as it traverses the list.

> **\|/**
> **ジ  Joe asks:**
> ## Should I Use Curry or Capture?
>
> I find curried functions easier to read, especially when chaining transformations. Capture syntax is more idiomatic in Elixir, but it can be brittle. As *Functional Programming: A PragPub Anthology [Sw17]* notes, Elixir only captures the nearest enclosing expression when using &, which can lead to unexpected behavior in more complex cases.

## Run It

Let's start by generating some Rides and Patrons:

```
iex> tea_cup = FunPark.Ride.make("Tea Cup")
iex> roller_mtn = FunPark.Ride.make("Roller Mountain", min_height: 120)
iex> haunted_mansion = FunPark.Ride.make("Haunted Mansion", min_age: 14)
iex> rides = [tea_cup, roller_mtn, haunted_mansion]

iex> alice = FunPark.Patron.make("Alice", 13, 150)
iex> beth = FunPark.Patron.make("Beth", 15, 110)
```

Alice is tall enough for Roller Mountain but not old enough for the Haunted Mansion. Her suggested rides include Tea Cup and Roller Mountain:

```
iex> alice |> FunPark.Ride.suggested_rides(rides)
[
  %FunPark.Ride{ name: "Tea Cup", ... },
  %FunPark.Ride{ name: "Roller Mountain", ... }
]
```

Beth meets the age requirement for Haunted Mansion but isn't tall enough for Roller Mountain. Her suggested rides include Tea Cup and Haunted Mansion:

```
iex> beth |> FunPark.Ride.suggested_rides(rides)
[
  %FunPark.Ride{ name: "Tea Cup", ... },
  %FunPark.Ride{ name: "Haunted Mansion", ... }
]
```

Later, the wait time for Tea Cup increases; Beth is no longer eligible:

```
iex> tea_cup = FunPark.Ride.change(tea_cup, %{wait_time: 40})
iex> rides = [tea_cup, roller_mtn, haunted_mansion]
iex> beth |> FunPark.Ride.suggested_rides(rides)
[
  %FunPark.Ride{ name: "Haunted Mansion", ... }
]
```

Because Elixir's Enum module works directly with predicates, we can express context-specific logic in collection operations—making it easy to adapt as the domain model evolves.

# Model the FastPass

Let's turn our attention to FastPass—specifically, the business rules that govern who gets fast lane access and under what conditions. These rules span three bounded contexts: Patron, FastPass, and Ride. The Patron manages the collection of passes, the FastPass defines what makes one valid, and the Ride determines access to the fast lane.

Later, we'll lift these same rules into monads for richer forms of validation. But everything starts here: simple predicates defining the domain.

### FastPass Management in the Patron Context

The Patron context is responsible for managing its collection of FastPasses. Let's define functions to add and remove a FastPass:

```
lib/fun_park/patron.ex
def add_fast_pass(%__MODULE__{} = patron, fast_pass) do
  fast_passes = List.union([fast_pass], get_fast_passes(patron))

  change(patron, %{fast_passes: fast_passes})
end
```

This updates through change/2, centralizing modifications, and uses Fun-Park.List.union/2 to ensure *idempotency*—the same action can be repeated without changing the result. Thanks to our Eq protocol, FunPark already knows how to deduplicate FastPasses.

Removing a FastPass is similar, but instead of union/2, we need difference/2:

```
lib/fun_park/patron.ex
def remove_fast_pass(%__MODULE__{} = patron, fast_pass) do
  fast_passes = List.difference(get_fast_passes(patron), [fast_pass])

  change(patron, %{fast_passes: fast_passes})
end
```

Like add_fast_pass/2, this is also idempotent; calling remove_fast_pass/2 multiple times with the same FastPass has no additional effect after the first removal.

## Run It

Let's start by generating a FassPass and a Patron:

```
iex> tea_cup = FunPark.Ride.make("Tea Cup")
iex> datetime = DateTime.new!(~D[2025-06-01], ~T[13:00:00])
iex> fast_pass = FunPark.FastPass.make(tea_cup, datetime)

iex> alice = FunPark.Patron.make("Alice", 13, 150)
%FunPark.Patron{ name: "Alice", fast_passes: [], ... }
```

Alice can add a FastPass for the Tea Cup ride:

```
iex> alice = FunPark.Patron.add_fast_pass(alice, fast_pass)
%FunPark.Patron{
  name: "Alice",
  fast_passes: [
    %FunPark.FastPass{ ride: %FunPark.Ride{ name: "Tea Cup", ... }, ... }
  ],
  ...
}
```

And she can remove it when it's no longer needed:

```
iex> alice = FunPark.Patron.remove_fast_pass(alice, fast_pass)
%FunPark.Patron{ name: "Alice", fast_passes: [], ... }
```

## Validity Rules in the FastPass Context

The FastPass context defines the rules for whether a pass is valid:

```
lib/fun_park/fast_pass.ex
def get_ride(%__MODULE__{ride: ride}), do: ride

def valid?(%__MODULE__{} = fast_pass, %Ride{} = ride) do
  Eq.Utils.eq?(get_ride(fast_pass), ride)
end
```

Here, get_ride/1 extracts the ride from the pass, and valid?/2 uses the Eq protocol to check whether it matches the given ride.

## Fast Lane Access

The Ride context determines whether a patron can enter the fast lane:

```
lib/fun_park/ride.ex
def fast_pass?(%Patron{} = patron, %__MODULE__{} = ride) do
  patron
  |> Patron.get_fast_passes()
  |> Enum.any?(&FastPass.valid?(&1, ride))
end
```

This extracts the patron's passes and uses Enum.any?/2 with FastPass.valid?/2 to check if any are valid for the given ride. Each context stays focused on its own concerns—Patron manages its passes, FastPass defines what makes a pass valid, and Ride determines access to the fast lane.

## Run It

Let's start by creating a Ride, a FastPass, and a Patron:

```
iex> haunted_mansion = FunPark.Ride.make("Haunted Mansion", min_age: 14)
iex> datetime = DateTime.new!(~D[2025-06-01], ~T[13:00:00])
iex> fast_pass = FunPark.FastPass.make(haunted_mansion, datetime)

iex> alice = FunPark.Patron.make("Alice", 13, 150)
```

Without a FastPass, Alice is not eligible for the Haunted Mansion:

```
iex> alice |> FunPark.Ride.fast_pass?(haunted_mansion)
false
```

Let's give her one:

```
iex> alice = FunPark.Patron.add_fast_pass(alice, fast_pass)
```

Now she's eligible:

```
iex> alice |> FunPark.Ride.fast_pass?(haunted_mansion)
true
```

But wait—after launch, the Ride expert reports a wave of guest complaints: patrons are being invited into the fast lane, only to be turned away as they attempt to board the ride. Alice had a valid FastPass but didn't meet the ride's eligibility requirements. Guests shouldn't be allowed into the fast lane for a ride they can't board. To fix this, we need to combine fast_pass?/2 and eligible?/2 to only allow patrons through who meet both conditions.

In complex domains, we learn as we go—refining our understanding and evolving the model to match. (The code for this is on the next page.)

```
def fast_pass_lane?(%Patron{} = patron, %__MODULE__{} = ride) do
  has_fast_pass = curry(&fast_pass?/2).(patron)
  is_eligible = curry(&eligible?/2).(patron)

  p_all([has_fast_pass, is_eligible]).(ride)
end
```

Here, we determine whether a patron can enter the fast lane by combining two conditions: they must have a valid FastPass, and they must be eligible to ride. Both fast_pass?/2 and eligible?/2 are curried with the patron, producing unary functions. These are passed to p_all/1, which composes them into a single predicate that returns true only if all conditions are satisfied for the given ride.

But just as we roll out the fix, another update comes in: VIP patrons don't need FastPasses at all, they always get fast lane access. We can extend the logic by adding a vip?/1 predicate in the Patron context and updating fast_pass_lane?/2 to allow VIPs or patrons who hold a valid FastPass and meet the ride's eligibility requirements.

lib/fun_park/patron.ex
```
def vip?(%__MODULE__{ticket_tier: :vip}), do: true
def vip?(%__MODULE__{}), do: false
```

## Well, That Got Complicated

Here's the catch: eligible?/2 takes two arguments—the Patron comes first, and the Ride comes second. When we use curry/1, it fills in arguments from left to right. Partially applying eligible?/2 with a Patron gives us a function that expects a Ride, which works well when composing over rides.

But vip?/1 takes only a Patron, not a Ride, so it doesn't fit into the same pipeline.

We could rewrite our functions to reverse the argument order, but that would introduce duplication. A better solution is to use curry_r/1, which applies arguments from right to left and returns a function that expects a Patron, making it compatible with vip?/1.

lib/fun_park/utils.ex
```
def curry_r(fun) when is_function(fun) do
  arity = :erlang.fun_info(fun, :arity) |> elem(1)
  curry_r(fun, arity, [])
end

defp curry_r(fun, 1, args),
  do: fn last_arg -> apply(fun, [last_arg | args]) end

defp curry_r(fun, arity, args) when arity > 1 do
  fn next_arg -> curry_r(fun, arity - 1, [next_arg | args]) end
end
```

Functional languages typically place the data structure as the last argument in a function. Elixir flips this pattern—placing the data first. This choice is reflected in its pipe operator, which applies input to the first argument rather than the more typical last. To support this flow, curry_r/1—which applies arguments from right to left—is often a better fit for Elixir's conventions.

Now we can update the fast lane logic:

```
lib/fun_park/ride.ex
def fast_pass_lane?(%Patron{} = patron, %__MODULE__{} = ride) do
  has_fast_pass = curry_r(&fast_pass?/2).(ride)
  is_eligible = curry_r(&eligible?/2).(ride)
  is_vip = &Patron.vip?/1

  p_all([is_eligible, p_any([is_vip, has_fast_pass])]).(patron)
end
```

By using curry_r/1, we apply the Ride first, then the Patron, which gives us (fast_pass OR vip) AND eligible—allowing only patrons who meet eligibility and either have a FastPass or VIP status.

Notice what's happening: you're no longer thinking in terms of low-level functions—you're composing with higher-level models. That's mastery in action—not just of functional programming but of the domain itself. Over time, these higher-level models become your team's shared vocabulary.

## Run It

Let's regenerate our Patrons, a Ride, and a FastPass:

```
iex> alice = FunPark.Patron.make("Alice", 13, 150)
iex> beth = FunPark.Patron.make("Beth", 15, 110)

iex> haunted_mansion = FunPark.Ride.make("Haunted Mansion", min_age: 14)
iex> datetime = DateTime.new!(~D[2025-06-01], ~T[13:00:00])
iex> fast_pass = FunPark.FastPass.make(haunted_mansion, datetime)
```

We'll give Alice a FastPass to the Haunted Mansion:

```
iex> alice = FunPark.Patron.add_fast_pass(alice, fast_pass)
```

Although Alice has a FastPass, she's too young to ride the Haunted Mansion. Meanwhile, Beth—who doesn't have a FastPass—is also ineligible for the fast lane. (The code is on the next page.)

```
iex> alice |> FunPark.Ride.fast_pass_lane?(haunted_mansion)
false
iex> beth |> FunPark.Ride.fast_pass_lane?(haunted_mansion)
false
```

Later, Beth upgrades her ticket. As a VIP, she's now eligible for the fast lane, even without a FastPass:

```
iex> beth = FunPark.Patron.change(beth, %{ticket_tier: :vip})
iex> beth |> FunPark.Ride.fast_pass_lane?(haunted_mansion)
true
```

By modeling FastPass as its own bounded context and treating Patron as a conformist, we keep responsibilities clear, allowing each part of the system to evolve independently as our understanding of the domain evolves.

## Fold Conditional Logic

We introduced Foldable, on page 49, where we saw how lists can be folded into a single result.

Predicates return either true or false, which gives them two distinct paths. This branching structure also makes them foldable. But unlike lists, predicates aren't ordered, so fold_l/3 and fold_r/3 behave the same.

lib/fun_park/predicate.ex
```
defimpl FunPark.Foldable, for: Function do
  def fold_l(predicate, true_func, false_func) do
    case predicate.() do
      true -> true_func.()
      false -> false_func.()
    end
  end

  def fold_r(predicate, true_func, false_func) do
    fold_l(predicate, true_func, false_func)
  end
end
```

### Run It

Let's start by generating the Tea Cup ride with a 100-minute wait:

```
iex> tea_cup = FunPark.Ride.make("Tea Cup", online: true, wait_time: 100)
%FunPark.Ride{name: "Tea Cup", online: true, wait_time: 100, ...}
```

Earlier, our Ride expert introduced suggested?/1, a predicate that returns true for rides that are online and have a wait under 30 minutes. With a 100-minute wait, the Tea Cup doesn't qualify:

```
iex> FunPark.Ride.suggested?(tea_cup)
false
```

We can fold the predicate result into a string, "Yes" or "No", using fold_l/3:

```
iex> yes_or_no = fn val, pred ->
  FunPark.Foldable.fold_l(fn ->
    pred.(val) end, fn -> "Yes" end, fn -> "No" end) end
```

This lets us convert branching logic into a single result.

```
iex> yes_or_no.(tea_cup, &FunPark.Ride.suggested?/1)
"No"
```

From the perspective of our label, the result is a string—it doesn't care what it says.

## Act on It

The Ride expert wants to improve the guest experience by offering more tailored suggestions. Currently, our suggested?/2 function takes a patron and a ride—it checks whether the patron is eligible, the ride is online, and the wait time is short. That's been working well.

But now, they'd like to factor in guest interests. Some visitors seek out :thrill rides, and others prefer :family-friendly options.

Right away, we notice this is cross-cutting logic, involving both Patron and Ride. Where does it belong? From a context mapping perspective, this is a customer/supplier relationship: the Ride context supplies tags, and the Patron context uses them to express preferences. That means the logic lives with Patron.

After consulting the Patron expert, the picture expands: guests don't just seek certain types of rides—they also avoid specific experiences, like :dark or :water. These preferences need to be respected as well.

Now that we have the right people in the room, we turn to the ubiquitous language. In the Ride context, a *suggested* ride means the guest is eligible and the ride is currently available. But in the Patron context, when they talk about a ride the guest is likely to enjoy, they call it *recommended*.

Find the Predicate Chapter Answers, on page 213.

## What You've Learned

Predicates do more than return true or false—they capture decisions, express domain meaning, and structure logic in modular, reusable ways. Because predicates follow the rules of Boolean logic, we can combine them with and, or, and not. Their composability reduces branching and lowers cyclomatic complexity, making logic easier to understand, test, and change as requirements shift.

Without clear boundaries, predicates can become scattered or duplicated across the system. Each predicate should live within its bounded context and reflect the ubiquitous language of its domain. When logic spans contexts—such as a patron needing to meet a ride's height requirement—context mapping helps keep responsibilities clear.

Elixir supports predicate composition, although its data-first style, multi-arity functions, and explicit higher-order calls can introduce friction.

Even if you go no further, you have Eq, Ord, Monoid, and Predicate—tools for expressing domain logic declaratively and shaping systems that evolve as your understanding deepens. You can stop here and apply them within imperative control flow or continue and learn monads, a declarative approach to control flow.

> Are you stuck? If yes, that's a good thing. Learning happens at the edge of what we can currently do. Bushwhacking through concepts we don't understand is how we build expertise. It's not a problem; it's the path.

# CHAPTER 6

# Compose in Context with Monads

Predicates define the business rules: is the ride online, are you tall enough, can you take the fast lane? But rules can't decide what happens next. For that, we need control flow—and in functional programming, that's a job for the monad.

Unlike predicates or monoids, which translate naturally from their mathematical foundations, monads in programming are *inspired* by category theory; they're not direct implementations of its mathematical counterpart.

So rather than diving into endofunctors, morphisms, and adjunctions, let's focus on what monads do in code: monads compose computations within a context.

Let's unpack that.

If you're coming from an imperative background, *compose* means building a concrete thing from reusable components. A car is composed of an engine and wheels. A UI is composed of buttons and views. The emphasis is on assembling parts into a structure. In this world, *context* refers to the surrounding environment—such as a database connection, the current user, or a configuration map. These are concrete, read-only values, injected, passed explicitly, or accessed through global state.

In functional programming, *compose* means combining behavior. Functions are composed to build a transformation—a new function whose behavior is defined by chaining smaller functions together. Functional programming patterns—Eq, Ord, Monoid, Predicate, and now Monad—are especially well-suited to this kind of composition.

Monads deal with context, but in a more abstract sense. Context can mean a read-only environment, modeled with the Reader monad. But it can also mean the context of absence (Maybe), the context of failure (Either), or the context of asynchronous computation (Effect).

You've used a monad without realizing it—in a list, where you compose computations within the context of an ordered sequence.

# Build the Monad

In his 1995 paper *Monads for Functional Programming*, Philip Wadler outlined two essential operations that comprise a monad: one applies to a transformation while preserving structure (map), and one chains context-aware computations (bind).[1] Today, most definitions of a monad support more than just these two—but they remain the foundation.

## Transform with a Functor

Anyone who has mapped over a list has used a functor. Each item is transformed, but the structure stays the same—returning the same number of items, in the same order.

More specifically, a functor follows two rules:

- *Identity:* Mapping with the identity function returns a copy of the original structure. map(fn x -> x end, F(a)) = F(a)

- *Composition:* Mapping in two steps is the same as mapping once with a composed function. map(f, map(g, F(a))) = map(fn x -> f.(g.(x)) end, F(a))

Let's see Elixir's Enum functor in action.

Our Patron expert introduces a new promotion that adds 10 points to a patron's reward_points.

```
lib/fun_park/patron.ex
def promotion(%__MODULE__{} = patron, points) do
  new_points = Math.sum(get_reward_points(patron), points)

  change(patron, %{reward_points: new_points})
end
```

This uses change/2 to apply a promotion by incrementing a patron's existing reward points.

### Run It

Start Elixir's iex and run mix.

```
iex -S mix
```

---

1.    https://homepages.inf.ed.ac.uk/wadler/papers/marktoberdorf/baastad.pdf

Let's start by generating a list of patrons:

```
iex> alice = FunPark.Patron.make("Alice", 14, 125, reward_points: 25)
iex> beth = FunPark.Patron.make("Beth", 15, 140, reward_points: 10)
iex> charles = FunPark.Patron.make("Charles", 13, 130, reward_points: 50)
iex> patrons = [alice, beth, charles]
```

With Elixir's Enum.map/2 functor, we can apply promotion/2 to each patron, adding 10 to their reward points.

```
iex> patrons |> Enum.map(&FunPark.Patron.promotion(&1, 10))
[
  %FunPark.Patron{name: "Alice", reward_points: 35, ...},
  %FunPark.Patron{name: "Beth", reward_points: 20, ...},
  %FunPark.Patron{name: "Charles", reward_points: 60, ...}
]
```

The functor applies the transformation to each element, preserving the list's structure. Its length and order remain unchanged.

## Sequence Computations

A monad includes behavior for chaining computations within a context. But unlike map, there's no universally agreed-upon name for this operation, so we'll follow Haskell's convention and call it bind.

The bind operation follows three laws:

- *Left identity:* Wrapping a value and then binding it to a function is the same as applying the function directly. bind(pure(a), f) = f(a)

- *Right identity:* Binding a monad to pure has no effect. bind(m, pure) = m

- *Associativity:* It doesn't matter how you nest your bindings—the result is the same. bind(bind(m, f), g) = bind(m, fn x -> bind(f(x), g) end)

These laws describe how bind behaves, but you don't need to memorize them. Their purpose is to ensure that chaining behaves predictably.

Elixir's Enum includes bind, but under the name flat_map/2.

### Run It

First, we need to define a *Kleisli function.* Named after Heinrich Kleisli, it's a function that takes an input and returns a monad.

```
kleisli_fn = fn x -> if rem(x, 2) == 0, do: [x * x], else: [] end
```

This Kleisli function takes a number and returns a list: the squared value for even numbers or an empty list for odd ones.

Next, we need a list of values:

```
list = [1, 2, 3, 4, 5, 6]
```

Let's apply our Kleisli function:

```
list |> Enum.flat_map(kleisli_fn)
[4, 16, 36]
```

We get a new list. Unlike map, bind allowed us to reshape the structure. We started with six items and ended with three.

map and bind are both context-aware—in this case, the context is a list. map transforms each item while preserving the structure; bind allows the structure to change.

Interestingly, the monad is not a static concept. Most modern formulations include a third block of logic called the applicative.[2]

## Independent Computations

Applicative is useful when we need to combine two things that are already inside a context. It follows four fundamental rules:

- *Identity:* Applying a wrapped identity function has no effect. ap(pure(fn x -> x end), F(a)) = F(a)

- *Homomorphism:* Lifting a function and a value separately is the same as applying them directly. ap(pure(f), pure(a)) = pure(f.(a))

- *Interchange:* A function in context can be applied to a pure value, or the value can be lifted into a function and applied to the context instead. ap(F(f), pure(a)) = ap(pure(fn g -> g.(a) end), F(f))

- *Composition:* Applying functions step by step inside the context behaves the same as applying them all at once. ap(ap(ap(pure(fn f -> fn g -> fn x -> f.(g.(x))) end, F(f)), F(g)), F(a)) = ap(F(f), ap(F(g), F(a)))

Uffda … that's a lot. But here's the heart of it: these rules make sure that applying functions in a context behaves just like it would outside the context.

Unlike map or bind, no applicative function exists in Elixir's Enum module.

---

2.   https://www.staff.city.ac.uk/~ross/papers/Applicative.html

However, we can make one:

**Run It**

```
ap = fn values, funcs -> for f <- funcs, v <- values, do: f.(v) end
```

Here, our ap/2 function works within the context of lists, taking a list of values and a list of functions and applying each function to every value—producing a new list of results.

Next, we need a couple of simple functions, add_one/1 and add_two/1:

```
add_one = fn x -> x + 1 end
add_two = fn x -> x + 2 end
func_list = [add_one, add_two]
```

We've assembled our functions into a list of functions.

And we need a list of values:

```
list = [10, 20, 30]
```

Finally, we use ap to apply our list of functions to our list of values:

```
list |> ap.(func_list)
[11, 21, 31, 12, 22, 32]
```

The result is a list of all calculations. Like bind, ap operates within a context—and can reshape the structure. Here, the output list is longer than the input because each function is applied to every value.

With bind, each step depends on the result of the previous one. With ap, each function is applied *independently* to each input, with no dependency between steps.

map transforms. bind chains. ap collects.

## The Protocol

To build monads in Elixir, we need a protocol.

```
lib/fun_park/monad.ex
defprotocol FunPark.Monad do
  def map(monad_value, func)
  def bind(monad_value, func_returning_monad)
  def ap(monadic_func, monad_value)
end
```

1. map/2 applies a function to a value in a context, preserving the structure.
2. bind/2 sequences computations, allowing each step to determine the next, all within the context.
3. ap/2 applies a function to a value, where both are in the same context.

## Model Neutrality with Identity

> **i** A production-ready Identity is available in the Funx library.[3]

The most basic function is the identity function—it returns its input unchanged. The same idea applies to monads: the simplest is the Identity monad. It wraps a value without adding any behavior—it's a neutral container that satisfies the monad laws.

```
lib/fun_park/monad/identity.ex
@enforce_keys [:value]
defstruct [:value]

def pure(value), do: %__MODULE__{value: value}
def extract(%__MODULE__{value: value}), do: value
```

The pure/1 function lifts a value into the Identity context, and extract/1 gets the contained value.

> ### Joe asks:
> ## Doesn't pure Belong with the Monad Protocol?
>
> If you come from a functional programming background, you expect pure/1 to sit alongside map/2, ap/2, and bind/2.
>
> But in Elixir, pure/1 doesn't carry enough information to know which monad to lift into. Instead, we define it in each monad's module—leaving it to the caller to choose the target context.

### Run It

Let's start by generating a Patron:

```
iex> alice = FunPark.Patron.make("Alice", 14, 130)
%FunPark.Patron{id: 1602, name: "Alice", ...}
```

---

3.  https://hexdocs.pm/funx/Funx.Monad.Identity.html

We can lift Alice into the Identity context:

```
iex> alice_monad = FunPark.Identity.pure(alice)
%FunPark.Identity{
  value: %FunPark.Patron{id: 1602, name: "Alice", ...}
}
```

And we can extract her:

```
iex> FunPark.Identity.extract(alice_monad)
%FunPark.Patron{id: 1602, name: "Alice", ...}
```

In fact, we can pass anything through the Identity monad with no effect:

```
iex> :apple |> FunPark.Identity.pure() |> FunPark.Identity.extract()
:apple
```

## Equality

Not all monads implement Eq, but many do, including Identity.

```
lib/fun_park/monad/identity.ex
defimpl FunPark.Eq, for: FunPark.Identity do
  alias FunPark.Identity
  alias FunPark.Eq

  def eq?(%Identity{value: v1}, %Identity{value: v2}), do: Eq.eq?(v1, v2)

  def not_eq?(%Identity{value: v1}, %Identity{value: v2}),
    do: Eq.not_eq?(v1, v2)
end
```

The Identity monad unwraps its contents and delegates to the Eq protocol.

### Run It

Let's start by generating a couple of patrons:

```
iex> alice = FunPark.Patron.make("Alice", 14, 130)
iex> beth = FunPark.Patron.make("Beth", 16, 125)
```

The Eq protocol knows when they are equivalent:

```
iex> FunPark.Eq.Utils.eq?(alice, alice)
true

iex> FunPark.Eq.Utils.eq?(alice, beth)
false
```

This is so even when they're wrapped in the Identity monad:

```
iex> alice_monad = FunPark.Identity.pure(alice)
iex> beth_monad = FunPark.Identity.pure(beth)

iex> FunPark.Eq.Utils.eq?(alice_monad, alice_monad)
true

iex> FunPark.Eq.Utils.eq?(alice_monad, beth_monad)
false
```

Here our Eq uses projection: the Identity implementation projects to the wrapped value, which delegates to the Eq implementation for Patron. That implementation, in turn, projects to the patron's ID. Each layer delegates by focusing on the part that defines equality in its context.

## Ordering

The Identity monad also implements Ord.

lib/fun_park/monad/identity.ex
```
defimpl FunPark.Ord, for: FunPark.Identity do
  alias FunPark.Ord
  alias FunPark.Identity

  def lt?(%Identity{value: v1}, %Identity{value: v2}), do: Ord.lt?(v1, v2)
  def le?(%Identity{value: v1}, %Identity{value: v2}), do: Ord.le?(v1, v2)
  def gt?(%Identity{value: v1}, %Identity{value: v2}), do: Ord.gt?(v1, v2)
  def ge?(%Identity{value: v1}, %Identity{value: v2}), do: Ord.ge?(v1, v2)
end
```

As with Eq, it unwraps its contents and delegates comparison to Ord.

### Run It

Again, let's generate our Patrons:

```
iex> alice = FunPark.Patron.make("Alice", 14, 135, ticket_tier: :vip)
iex> beth = FunPark.Patron.make("Beth", 16, 125)
```

The Patron context's default ordering is by name, so Alice is less than Beth:

```
iex> FunPark.Ord.Utils.compare(alice, beth)
:lt
```

It makes no difference if they are wrapped in Identity monads:

```
iex> alice_monad = FunPark.Identity.pure(alice)
iex> beth_monad = FunPark.Identity.pure(beth)
iex> FunPark.Ord.Utils.compare(alice_monad, beth_monad)
:lt
```

Like Eq, Ord composes through projection, keeping our logic modular, composable, and easy to extend.

## Lift Eq and Order

Identity delegates to the default Eq and Ord implementations of its contents. But to use custom comparators, we need to explicitly lift them into the context.

lib/fun_park/monad/identity.ex
```
def lift_eq(custom_eq) do
  custom_eq = Eq.Utils.to_eq_map(custom_eq)

  %{
    eq?: fn
      %__MODULE__{value: a}, %__MODULE__{value: b} -> custom_eq.eq?.(a, b)
    end,
    not_eq?: fn
      %__MODULE__{value: a}, %__MODULE__{value: b} ->
        custom_eq.not_eq?.(a, b)
    end
  }
end
```

For lift_eq/1, the returned eq?/2 and not_eq?/2 functions unwrap the values from the Identity structs and apply the corresponding functions from custom_eq.

lib/fun_park/monad/identity.ex
```
def lift_ord(custom_ord) do
  custom_ord = Ord.Utils.to_ord_map(custom_ord)

  %{
    lt?: fn
      %__MODULE__{value: v1}, %__MODULE__{value: v2} ->
        custom_ord.lt?.(v1, v2)
    end,
    le?: fn
      %__MODULE__{value: v1}, %__MODULE__{value: v2} ->
        custom_ord.le?.(v1, v2)
    end,
    gt?: fn
      %__MODULE__{value: v1}, %__MODULE__{value: v2} ->
        custom_ord.gt?.(v1, v2)
    end,
    ge?: fn
      %__MODULE__{value: v1}, %__MODULE__{value: v2} ->
        custom_ord.ge?.(v1, v2)
    end
  }
end
```

For lift_ord/1, each returned function unwraps the values from the Identity structs and delegates directly to the matching functions in custom_ord.

### Run It

Let's return to our patrons:

```
iex> alice = FunPark.Patron.make("Alice", 14, 135, ticket_tier: :vip)
iex> beth = FunPark.Patron.make("Beth", 16, 125)
```

We have custom ordering based on priority:

```
iex> priority_ord = FunPark.Patron.ord_by_priority()
```

Within the context of priority, Alice—with her VIP status—is greater than Beth.

```
iex> FunPark.Ord.Utils.compare(alice, beth, priority_ord)
:gt
```

We can lift that priority_ord into the Identity context:

```
iex> lifted_priority_ord = FunPark.Identity.lift_ord(priority_ord)
```

And we get the same result for our wrapped patrons:

```
iex> alice_monad = FunPark.Identity.pure(alice)
iex> beth_monad = FunPark.Identity.pure(beth)

iex> FunPark.Ord.Utils.compare(alice_monad, beth_monad, lifted_priority_ord)
:gt
```

By lifting the comparator, we're adapting our domain-specific logic to operate within the Identity context.

## Monadic Logic

And of course, the Identity monad implements the Monad protocol:

```
lib/fun_park/monad/identity.ex
defimpl FunPark.Monad, for: FunPark.Identity do
  alias FunPark.Identity

  def map(%Identity{value: value}, func) do
    Identity.pure(func.(value))
  end

  def bind(%Identity{value: value}, func) do
    func.(value)
  end
```

```
  def ap(%Identity{value: func}, %Identity{value: value}) do
    Identity.pure(func.(value))
  end
end
```

- map/2 unwraps the value from the Identity, applies the function, and rewraps
  the result.
- bind/2 unwraps the value from the Identity and applies it to the provided
  function, which must return a new Identity.
- ap/2 unwraps both the function and the value, applies the function to the
  value, and rewraps the result.

Let's return to our Ride expert's wait time issue. Wait times aren't set
once—they're updated continuously by multiple sensors tracking queue
movement and ride cycles. Instead of replacing the value with each update,
we need to accumulate them.

lib/fun_park/ride.ex
```
def add_wait_time(
      %__MODULE__{wait_time: wait_time} = ride,
      minutes
    )
    when is_number(minutes) and minutes > 0 do
  change(ride, %{wait_time: Math.sum(wait_time, minutes)})
end
```

The add_wait_time/2 function takes a ride and a number of minutes, ensuring
the minutes are positive. It uses the ride's change/2 function to increment the
current wait time by the given amount.

### Run It

Let's generate the Tea Cup ride:

```
iex> tea_cup = FunPark.Ride.make("Tea Cup", wait_time: 10)
%FunPark.Ride{ name: "Tea Cup", wait_time: 10, ... }
```

We can add 20 minutes:

```
iex> FunPark.Ride.add_wait_time(tea_cup, 20)
%FunPark.Ride{ name: "Tea Cup", wait_time: 30, ... }
```

And because add_wait_time/2 is closed under its operation, we can use the pipe
operator to compose multiple sensors (code on next page):

```
iex> tea_cup
  |> FunPark.Ride.add_wait_time(20)
  |> FunPark.Ride.add_wait_time(10)
  |> FunPark.Ride.add_wait_time(5)
%FunPark.Ride{ name: "Tea Cup", wait_time: 45, ... }
```

The same applies within the Identity context. First, let's lift the Tea Cup ride:

```
iex> tea_cup_m = FunPark.Identity.pure(tea_cup)
%FunPark.Identity{
  value: %FunPark.Ride{ name: "Tea Cup", wait_time: 10, ... }
}
```

To make things easier, we'll curry the add_wait_time/2 function:

```
iex> add_wait = FunPark.Utils.curry_r(&FunPark.Ride.add_wait_time/2)
```

Now we can apply it to the monad using map/2:

```
iex> FunPark.Monad.map(tea_cup_m, add_wait.(20))
%FunPark.Identity{
  value: %FunPark.Ride{ name: "Tea Cup", wait_time: 30, ... }
}
```

And again, we can compose updates from three sensors:

```
iex> tea_cup_m
  |> FunPark.Monad.map(add_wait.(20))
  |> FunPark.Monad.map(add_wait.(10))
  |> FunPark.Monad.map(add_wait.(5))
%FunPark.Identity{
  value: %FunPark.Ride{ name: "Tea Cup", wait_time: 45, ... }
}
```

The monad's map/2 applies add_wait_time/2 to the ride inside the Identity context, transforming the value while preserving the structure.

The bind/2 function differs in one key way: it lets each step choose the structure of the result. In monads with multiple structures—like Maybe or Either—bind can switch between them. But Identity has only one structure, so there's nothing to switch to.

Even so, we can model our sensors so they choose the structure:

```
iex> sensor_1 = &FunPark.Identity.pure(add_wait.(10).(&1))
iex> sensor_2 = &FunPark.Identity.pure(add_wait.(5).(&1))
iex> sensor_3 = &FunPark.Identity.pure(add_wait.(20).(&1))
```

Our sensors are now Kleisli functions. They take an input and return an Identity monad. We chain Kleisli functions with bind/2:

```
iex> tea_cup_m
|> FunPark.Monad.bind(sensor_1)
|> FunPark.Monad.bind(sensor_2)
|> FunPark.Monad.bind(sensor_3)
%FunPark.Identity{
  value: %FunPark.Ride{ name: "Tea Cup", wait_time: 45, ...}
}
```

Monads themselves aren't closed, but their core operations are. Functions like map/2, bind/2, and ap/2 return a result in the same monadic context, allowing us to pipe them together.

So what are we gaining by using Identity? Normally, you wouldn't bother wrapping something transparently. But with a sensor, you might: sensors sit outside the program, and by nature, they can fail. While our expert hasn't raised that concern yet, we might want to get ahead of the curve by starting with Identity now, with the idea that we might later elevate the context to handle missing sensors (Maybe) or failing sensors (Either).

## What You've Learned

Through the list monad, we saw how monadic operations shape control flow. map keeps structure intact. bind chains computations. ap applies functions independently across inputs. These mental models form the building blocks for mastery, and we'll extend them as we explore other monads.

Identity isn't interesting for its context—it has none. But it shows how other abstractions, such as Eq and Ord, can be lifted into a monad. Monads don't just define operations; they define how *other* abstractions behave in their context.

Monads make control flow explicit, isolate effects, and keep decisions local.

We'll move from the Identity monad to Reader, a monad for shared context. Where Identity simply carries a result, Reader threads an environment through a deferred computation.

> This chapter introduced several core ideas. It's okay if they don't all click right away. Mastery takes practice, not just exposure. As you continue into Reader and Maybe, you'll have chances to revisit and apply them. And remember, the LLM Tutor is always available to answer questions and test your understanding.[4]

---

4.  https://www.funxlib.com/tutor.html

# Access Shared Environment with Reader

A production-ready Reader is available in the Funx library.[1]

You already know many forms of control flow: branching with if/else or case; looping with for, while, or reduce; exiting early with return, break, or throw; and recovering with defaults, fallbacks, or catch blocks. In the last chapter, we saw how monads express control flow: map for transformation, bind for sequencing, and ap for collection.

Now we introduce another kind of control flow: deferred computation—define now, run later.

You've likely seen this before: callbacks that wait for events, or curried functions that wait for arguments. Once you internalize the mental model, you'll start to recognize it in more advanced designs like dependency injection and middleware pipelines.

Sometimes we need to defer computation *and* give it an environment—some shared state or behavior it can read from. In functional programming, that's the role of the Reader monad.

The Reader context, like Identity, has a single structure. It doesn't branch—it just passes data through. What it adds is read-only access to a shared environment.

The key to Reader is that it's lazy: it describes the steps for computing a result, but nothing happens until the environment is supplied.

---

1.   https://hexdocs.pm/funx/Funx.Monad.Reader.html

## Build the Structures

It has a pure/1 like Identity, but instead of extract/1, Reader uses run/2:

```
lib/fun_park/monad/reader.ex
@enforce_keys [:run]
defstruct [:run]

def pure(value), do: %__MODULE__{run: fn _env -> value end}

def run(%__MODULE__{run: f}, env), do: f.(env)
```

In Identity, pure/1 stores the value directly. In Reader, pure/1 wraps the logic in a *thunk*—a function that defers computation until the environment is available. When run/2 is called, it invokes the thunk, injecting the environment and returning the result.

## Monad Behaviors

To implement the monadic behaviors for Reader, we define map/2, bind/2, and ap/2:

```
lib/fun_park/monad/reader.ex
defimpl FunPark.Monad, for: FunPark.Reader do
  alias FunPark.Reader

  def map(%Reader{run: f}, func),
    do: %Reader{run: fn env -> func.(f.(env)) end}

  def bind(%Reader{run: f}, func),
    do: %Reader{run: fn env -> func.(f.(env)).run.(env) end}

  def ap(%Reader{run: f_func}, %Reader{run: f_value}),
    do: %Reader{run: fn env -> f_func.(env).(f_value.(env)) end}
end
```

The monadic functions behave like those of Identity, but behind the scenes, the Reader threads the environment through each step.

asks/1 is Reader's special sauce:

```
lib/fun_park/monad/reader.ex
def asks(func), do: %__MODULE__{run: func}
```

It allows functions within the context to access the read-only copy of the environment.

Let's see how the Reader solves common problems like prop drilling, dependency injection, and shared configuration.

# Avoid Prop Drilling

Some values need to be available deep in a computation, even if only one function uses them. Let's see what happens when we pass that information manually—and how Reader provides a structured alternative.

### Run It

Start Elixir's iex shell and run the mix script to compile the code and load the project.

```
iex -S mix
```

First, let's generate a patron and a value:

```
iex> alice = FunPark.Patron.make("Alice", 15, 130)
%FunPark.Patron{ name: "Alice", ... }

iex> value = 2
2
```

And we'll define a couple of simple functions:

```
iex> square = fn n -> n * n end
iex> message = fn {n, patron} -> "#{patron.name} has #{n}" end
```

We can call each one on its own:

```
iex> square.(value)
4

iex> message.({value, alice})
"Alice has 2"
```

But how do we compose them? It's not an arity problem—they're both arity-1. It's an information problem: square/1 just needs a number, but message/1 needs both a number and a patron.

One strategy is to tunnel, having the square/1 accept and forward the patron information:

```
iex> square_tunnel = fn {n, patron} -> {square.(n), patron} end
```

Now they can be piped together:

```
iex> {value, alice} |> square_tunnel.() |> message.()
"Alice has 4"
```

But passing information through functions that don't need it—commonly known as prop drilling—is widely considered an anti-pattern.

Instead, let's update our message/1 function to take the number and retrieve the patron from the Reader:

```
reader_message = fn n -> FunPark.Reader.asks(
  fn patron -> "#{patron.name} has #{n}" end
) end
```

Now we can build the pipeline:

```
iex> deferred_message = FunPark.Reader.pure(value)
|> FunPark.Monad.map(square)
|> FunPark.Monad.bind(reader_message)

%FunPark.Reader{
  run: #Function<...>
}
```

The Reader monad holds a suspended computation—a set of directions waiting for an environment. It doesn't run right away; it describes what to do once the environment is supplied.

We use run/2 to resolve deferred_message with Alice:

```
iex> FunPark.Reader.run(deferred_message, alice)
"Alice has 4"
```

And we can just as easily switch patrons:

```
iex> beth = FunPark.Patron.make("Beth", 16, 135)
%FunPark.Patron{ name: "Beth", ... }

iex> FunPark.Reader.run(deferred_message, beth)
"Beth has 4"
```

Here, we swapped Alice for Beth.

## Dependency Injection

Dependency injection decouples a component from its service, making it possible to swap implementations—such as testing versus production—without modifying the component.

### Run It

Let's start again with Alice:

```
iex> alice = FunPark.Patron.make("Alice", 15, 130)
```

We'll define two services: one for production and one for testing.

```
iex> prod_service = fn name -> "Hi, #{name}, from prod!" end
iex> test_service = fn name -> "Hi, #{name}, from test!" end
```

The deferred_greeting function applies a patron's name to the injected service:

```
iex> deferred_greeting = fn p -> FunPark.Reader.asks(& &1.(p.name)) end
```

Now we can construct a deferred greeting for Alice:

```
iex> alice_greeting = deferred_greeting.(alice)
%FunPark.Reader{
  run: #Function<...>
}
```

And we can inject the test service:

```
iex> FunPark.Reader.run(alice_greeting, test_service)
"Hi, Alice, from test!"
```

We can also inject the production service:

```
iex> FunPark.Reader.run(alice_greeting, prod_service)
"Hi, Alice, from prod!"
```

The essence of dependency injection is that the logic stays fixed while the environment varies. Here, we injected different services—test or production—without changing the function. This isolates domain logic from infrastructure concerns, making it easier to evolve.

## Shared Configuration

The Reader is also well suited for accessing configuration data—such as API keys, feature flags, or endpoint URLs—allowing us to pass data alongside computation without wiring it through every function.

A ride's configuration is an example of shared context. In practice, it would be stored in a database and reused across multiple systems, such as signage, access control, and reservations.

Our Ride factory can build a ride from configuration, using asks/1 to retrieve values from the environment.

```
lib/fun_park/ride.ex
def make_from_env(name) do
  FunPark.Reader.asks(fn config ->
    make(name)
    |> change(%{
      min_age: Map.get(config, :min_age, 0),
      min_height: Map.get(config, :min_height, 0)
    })
  end)
end
```

By abstracting configuration, we decouple unrelated parts of the system. Signage, access control, and reservations can all operate on the same rules—without needing to know how a Ride is built.

### Run It

Our Apple Cart ride has a configuration:

```
apple_config = %{min_age: 10, min_height: 120}
```

And we can create a deferred_apple—a ride that waits for its configuration:

```
deferred_apple = FunPark.Ride.make_from_env("Apple Cart")
%FunPark.Reader{run: #Function<...>}
```

Using the Reader, we run the deferred ride with its config:

```
apple = FunPark.Reader.run(deferred_apple, apple_config)
%FunPark.Ride{name: "Apple Cart", min_age: 10, min_height: 120, ...}
```

This keeps configuration decoupled from logic. The ride knows how to apply shared rules but not how they're delivered—preserving a clean boundary between domain behavior and infrastructure.

## What You've Learned

In object-oriented programming, prop drilling, dependency injection, and configuration sharing are treated as separate concerns, each with its own solution. In functional programming, they're all variations of the same idea: deferring access to a required input. The Reader monad addresses them with a single abstraction.

Notice what's missing from the Reader. Identity has a concept of equality (Eq) and order (Ord)—but Reader doesn't. Its context is deferred computation; there's no meaningful way to compare Reader monads without running them. Within the Reader context, equality isn't missing—it doesn't exist.

In the next chapter, we'll look at Maybe, a monad that introduces branching behavior. The Maybe context has two forms: one for something, and another for nothing.

Don't worry if Reader doesn't fully land yet. You'll see it again in the Effect monad, where you'll have an opportunity to apply it in a more concrete setting.

# CHAPTER 8

# Manage Absence with Maybe

> A production-ready Maybe is available in the Funx library.[1]

Identity and Reader follow a single path. But Maybe is quantum: not a value, but the possibility of one.

If you've written defensive code—null checks, guards, or defaults—you've encountered the quantum problem. Defensive code is often repetitive and scattered, but worse, it obscures domain intent. Is that input truly quantized, or was that check added "just in case"?

Maybe, like all monads, implements control flow within its context: it branches when something is missing, exits early when there's nothing to process, and recovers when possible. Maybe even extends to lists, enabling loops over collections of quantized values.

And like the other mental models we've explored, Maybe becomes more powerful once internalized. You'll start to recognize it in more sophisticated settings, such as continuous integration (CI) pipelines, graceful degradation, and authentication workflows.

As we work through Maybe, we'll also uncover a broader mental model: *make illegal states unrepresentable*. Instead of defending against mistakes, we can make them structurally impossible.

Let's get started.

---

1.  https://hexdocs.pm/funx/Funx.Monad.Maybe.html

## Build the Structures

The Maybe context has two structures, Just for the presence and Nothing for the absence.

### Just

Like Identity, Just contains a value.

```
lib/fun_park/monad/maybe/just.ex
defmodule FunPark.Monad.Maybe.Just do
  @enforce_keys [:value]
  defstruct [:value]

  def pure(nil), do: raise(ArgumentError, "Cannot wrap nil in a Just")
  def pure(value), do: %__MODULE__{value: value}
end
```

Just also enforces the presence of a value at construction, raising an error if given nil. After all, it doesn't make sense to have *just nothing*.

### Nothing

Nothing contains no value:

```
lib/fun_park/monad/maybe/nothing.ex
defmodule FunPark.Monad.Maybe.Nothing do
  defstruct []

  def pure, do: %__MODULE__{}
end
```

All monads include pure—in this case, a function lifting into Just or Nothing.

### Maybe

Next, we need a Maybe module to manage the distinction between Just and Nothing:

```
lib/fun_park/monad/maybe.ex
def just(value), do: Just.pure(value)
def nothing, do: Nothing.pure()
def pure(value), do: just(value)

def just?(%Just{}), do: true
def just?(_), do: false

def nothing?(%Nothing{}), do: true
def nothing?(_), do: false
```

The just/1 and nothing/0 helpers delegate to each module's pure function. pure/1 is an alias for Just.pure/1, reflecting that Maybe is biased toward Just.

We introduced the idea of *bias* back in the monoid chapter and revisited it in the predicate chapter. Conjunction assumes success and short-circuits on failure. Branching monads carry the same bias—Maybe assumes presence, diverting when something is absent.

Finally, just?/1 and nothing?/1 are *refinement* predicates, used to check whether we're in the Just or Nothing branch.

### Run It

Start Elixir's iex shell and run the mix script to compile the code and load the project.

```
iex -S mix
```

Let's start with one value from each branch:

```
iex> just_a = FunPark.Monad.Maybe.just("A")
%FunPark.Monad.Maybe.Just{value: "A"}

iex> nothing = FunPark.Monad.Maybe.nothing()
%FunPark.Monad.Maybe.Nothing{}
```

We can determine which branch we're in using a refinement:

```
iex> FunPark.Monad.Maybe.just?(just_a)
true

iex> FunPark.Monad.Maybe.nothing?(just_a)
false
```

Refinements extract the structural logic from a Maybe, transforming Just or None into a predicate true or false. They're especially useful in imperative code, where they can plug directly into if/else control flow.

A more declarative approach is to fold.

## Fold Branches

Maybe, with its quantum *possibility* of a value, remains unresolved until observed.

Folding is our act of observation: if the branch is Just, we pass the value to just_fn; if it's Nothing, we call the nothing_fn thunk to produce a fallback. Folding collapses the quantized structure into a single result.

```
defimpl FunPark.Foldable, for: FunPark.Monad.Maybe do
  alias FunPark.Monad.Maybe.{Just, Nothing}
```

```
  def fold_l(%Just{value: value}, just_fn, _nothing_fn),
    do: just_fn.(value)

  def fold_l(%Nothing{}, _just_fn, nothing_fn), do: nothing_fn.()

  def fold_r(%Just{value: value}, just_fn, _nothing_fn),
    do: just_fn.(value)

  def fold_r(%Nothing{}, _just_fn, nothing_fn), do: nothing_fn.()
end
```

## Not So Fast There, Bub

Elixir's protocols operate on structs, but Maybe isn't a struct—it's a sum type made up of the Just and Nothing structs. To implement the Foldable protocol, we define the behavior for each branch separately.

If Just, folding applies the higher-order transformation function to the contained value:

lib/fun_park/monad/maybe/just.ex
```
defimpl FunPark.Foldable, for: FunPark.Monad.Maybe.Just do
  alias FunPark.Monad.Maybe.Just

  def fold_l(%Just{value: value}, just_func, _nothing_func) do
    just_func.(value)
  end

  def fold_r(%Just{} = just, just_func, nothing_func) do
    fold_l(just, just_func, nothing_func)
  end
end
```

If Nothing, folding returns the result of the higher-order nothing_func/0 function:

lib/fun_park/monad/maybe/nothing.ex
```
defimpl FunPark.Foldable, for: FunPark.Monad.Maybe.Nothing do
  alias FunPark.Monad.Maybe.Nothing

  def fold_l(%Nothing{}, _just_func, nothing_func) do
    nothing_func.()
  end

  def fold_r(%Nothing{} = nothing, just_func, nothing_func) do
    fold_l(nothing, just_func, nothing_func)
  end
end
```

Together, these define the foldable behavior of Maybe.

## Run It

Let's return to our Ride expert's sensor problem. A ride's wait time is based on multiple sensors—but sensors exist outside the program, which means they can fail. To capture this uncertainty, we can lift each sensor into a Maybe, where it returns either *just* a number or *nothing* at all.

```
iex> good = FunPark.Monad.Maybe.just(10)
%FunPark.Monad.Maybe.Just{value: 10}

iex> bad = FunPark.Monad.Maybe.nothing()
%FunPark.Monad.Maybe.Nothing{}
```

Then fold to extract the result:

```
iex> FunPark.Foldable.fold_l(good, &"Sensor: #{&1}", fn -> "Broken" end)
"Sensor: 10"

iex> FunPark.Foldable.fold_l(bad, &"Sensor: #{&1}", fn -> "Broken" end)
"Broken"
```

Here, we've collapsed two distinct possibilities—*just* a number or *nothing*—into a single outcome: a string representing the sensor status.

## Default Value

Our Ride expert brings us an issue: when it comes to wait time, some information is better than none. Even with unreliable sensors, we need to report a wait time. In our case, flaky sensors should default to five minutes.

In the Maybe context, replacing *nothing* with a default is common enough to warrant a standalone get_or_else/2 function:

```
lib/fun_park/monad/maybe.ex
def get_or_else(maybe, default) do
  fold_l(maybe, fn value -> value end, fn -> default end)
end
```

This abstracts fold_l/3. For Just we apply the identity function. For Nothing we pass a thunk that returns the default value.

## Run It

Let's start by generating some flaky sensors:

```
iex> sensor_a = FunPark.Monad.Maybe.pure(20)
iex> sensor_b = FunPark.Monad.Maybe.nothing()
iex> sensor_c = FunPark.Monad.Maybe.pure(30)
iex> sensor_d = FunPark.Monad.Maybe.pure(5)
```

Now we can use the higher-level get_or_else/2:

```
iex> get_or_else_5 = &FunPark.Monad.Maybe.get_or_else(&1, 5)
```

Here, get_or_else_5/1 folds Maybe a number into a number. Since Math.sum/2 is closed over numbers, we can pipe the results together:

```
iex> get_or_else_5.(sensor_a)
|> FunPark.Math.sum(get_or_else_5.(sensor_b))
|> FunPark.Math.sum(get_or_else_5.(sensor_c))
|> FunPark.Math.sum(get_or_else_5.(sensor_d))
60
```

Even with unreliable data, we get a consistent and useful wait time.

# Lift Other Contexts

The pure/1 function lifts a value into the Maybe context. But sometimes we start from a different context. In those cases, we need to transform—or *lift*—the original context into Maybe.

### Identity

An Identity can be lifted into Maybe by pattern matching on nil—non-nil values become *just* that value, while nil becomes *nothing*:

```
lib/fun_park/monad/maybe.ex
def lift_identity(%Identity{} = identity) do
  case identity do
    %Identity{value: nil} -> nothing()
    %Identity{value: value} -> just(value)
  end
end
```

### Run It

Let's say we're dealing with a person whose name might be missing (nil):

```
iex> person_1 = FunPark.Identity.pure("Dave")
%FunPark.Identity{value: "Dave"}

iex> person_2 = FunPark.Identity.pure(nil)
%FunPark.Identity{value: nil}
```

Our lift_identity/1 logic converts this to a Maybe:

```
iex> maybe_person_1 = FunPark.Monad.Maybe.lift_identity(person_1)
%FunPark.Monad.Maybe.Just{value: "Dave"}

iex> maybe_person_2 = FunPark.Monad.Maybe.lift_identity(person_2)
%FunPark.Monad.Maybe.Nothing{}
```

And we can fold that Maybe back into a string:

```
iex> FunPark.Monad.Maybe.get_or_else(maybe_person_1, "Missing")
"Dave"

iex> FunPark.Monad.Maybe.get_or_else(maybe_person_2, "Missing")
"Missing"
```

Here, we've removed nil—a sentinel—and replaced it with a default.

But Maybe isn't just about handling missing values; it's about modeling intent.

Instead of guarding against failure, we can design it out!

## Predicate

Lifting a predicate is where Maybe starts to get interesting, shifting from a generic wrapper to a tool for narrowing context. A predicate captures a business rule, such as "this patron is a VIP." By lifting that rule, we refine the context to the *possibility* of a VIP patron (MaybeVipPatron), where values are either *just* VIP patrons or *nothing*.

In domain-driven design, structure reflects meaning. Refining a Patron to a Maybe-VipPatron doesn't just handle absence, it encodes a rule: only VIPs proceed. In functional programming, this is the principle of *Make illegal states unrepresentable*, a phrase popularized by Scott Wlaschin in *Domain Modeling Made Functional* *[Wla18]*. Non-VIPs are excluded from the context entirely, eliminating the need for defensive checks by making incorrect behavior structurally impossible.

We can fold the predicate to lift it into the Maybe context:

```
lib/fun_park/monad/maybe.ex
def lift_predicate(value, predicate) when is_function(predicate, 1) do
  fold_l(
    fn -> predicate.(value) end,
    fn -> just(value) end,
    fn -> nothing() end
  )
end
```

The lift_predicate/2 function uses fold_l/3, returning *just* the value if the predicate passes or *nothing* if it fails. From a domain-driven design perspective, it's refining the context according to a business rule.

## Run It

Let's start by generating the Tea Cup ride with a wait time of 100 minutes:

```
iex> tea_cup = FunPark.Ride.make("Tea Cup", online: true, wait_time: 100)
%FunPark.Ride{ name: "Tea Cup", online: true, wait_time: 100, ...}
```

Earlier, our Ride expert introduced suggested?/1, a predicate that checks whether a ride is online and has a wait time under 30 minutes. With a 100-minute wait, the Tea Cup is not suggested:

```
iex> FunPark.Ride.suggested?(tea_cup)
false
```

But instead of returning a Boolean, we can lift suggested?/1 into Maybe, refining the Ride context to a MaybeSuggestedRide—closed under the uncertainty of being suggested: it's *just* suggested or *nothing.*

Because the Tea Cup's wait time is too long, it becomes *nothing* in the new context:

```
iex> FunPark.Monad.Maybe.lift_predicate(tea_cup, &FunPark.Ride.suggested?/1)
%FunPark.Monad.Maybe.Nothing{}
```

Later, the wait time drops:

```
iex> tea_cup = FunPark.Ride.update_wait_time(tea_cup, 10)
%FunPark.Ride{ name: "Tea Cup", online: true, wait_time: 10, ... }
```

Now, the Tea Cup is *just* a SuggestedRide:

```
iex> FunPark.Monad.Maybe.lift_predicate(tea_cup, &FunPark.Ride.suggested?/1)
%FunPark.Monad.Maybe.Just{
  value: %FunPark.Ride{ name: "Tea Cup", online: true, wait_time: 10, ... }
}
```

By lifting the predicate into the Maybe context, we've moved from checking conditions to refining structure, ensuring that only rides meeting the criteria exist within the SuggestedRide context.

# Bridge Elixir Patterns

> *Are you crazy? We don't have time for some philosophical Functional Programming rewrite!*
>
> —Every team under a deadline, ever
>
> Interops let you *cut in*—drop into FP, chain a few operations, then cut back to idiomatic Elixir. No rewrites. No purity pledges.

Elixir provides common patterns for handling missing information, such as using nil or raising exceptions. We use *interop* functions to bridge these patterns with our functional abstractions.

For example, we can move between Elixir's nil and Maybe:

lib/fun_park/monad/maybe.ex
```
def from_nil(nil), do: nothing()
def from_nil(value), do: just(value)

def to_nil(%Nothing{}), do: nil
def to_nil(%Just{value: value}), do: value
```

Here, from_nil/1 transforms values that might be nil into our Maybe context, and to_nil/1 reverses the transformation. When possible, interops should be *isomorphic*, preserving all information as they move between representations.

Our Ride expert needs to update some business logic. Instead of simply checking whether a patron has a valid FastPass, we now need to retrieve the pass. We're shifting from a rule to control flow, from yes/no to the *possibility* of a valid FastPass.

lib/fun_park/ride.ex
```
def get_fast_pass(%Patron{} = patron, %__MODULE__{} = ride) do
  Enum.find(
    Patron.get_fast_passes(patron),
    &FastPass.valid?(&1, ride)
  )
  |> Maybe.from_nil()
end
```

Here, we use Elixir's Enum.find/2, which returns a matching value or nil. The from_nil/1 function lifts that result into the Maybe monad.

Instead of working in a FastPass context, we've shifted to MaybeValidFastPass—the possibility of a valid FastPass. In this context, absence is explicit, so there's no need to guard against the nil sentinel.

## Run It

Let's start by creating a Ride, FastPass, and Patron:

```
iex> haunted_mansion = FunPark.Ride.make("Haunted Mansion", min_age: 14)

iex> datetime = DateTime.new!(~D[2025-06-01], ~T[13:00:00])
iex> fast_pass = FunPark.FastPass.make(haunted_mansion, datetime)

iex> alice = FunPark.Patron.make("Alice", 13, 150)
```

Alice does not have a ValidFastPass, so the result is *nothing*:

```
iex> FunPark.Ride.get_fast_pass(alice, haunted_mansion)
%FunPark.Monad.Maybe.Nothing{}
```

Say she collects a FastPass for the Haunted Mansion:

```
iex> alice = FunPark.Patron.add_fast_pass(alice, fast_pass)
```

She now has *just* a ValidFastPass:

```
iex> FunPark.Ride.get_fast_pass(alice, haunted_mansion)
%FunPark.Monad.Maybe.Just{
  value: %FunPark.FastPass{
    ride: %FunPark.Ride{
      name: "Haunted Mansion",
      ...
    },
    time: ~U[2025-06-01 13:00:00Z]
  }
}
```

Interop functions draw a boundary around functional logic. Inside, we get the benefits of functional patterns—structure, composability, and local reasoning. Outside, we stay fluent in Elixir, free to use familiar libraries and conventions.

Next, let's look at how Maybe defines equality in the context of presence and absence.

## Define Equality

Earlier, we saw that monads define how other abstractions behave within their context. The Eq abstraction wasn't interesting in the Identity monad, which has no behavior, but it becomes meaningful in Maybe.

To implement Eq in the context of Maybe, we need to define what equality means for each structure:

lib/fun_park/monad/maybe/just.ex
```
defimpl FunPark.Eq, for: FunPark.Monad.Maybe.Just do
  alias FunPark.Monad.Maybe.{Just, Nothing}
  alias FunPark.Eq

  def eq?(%Just{value: v1}, %Just{value: v2}), do: Eq.eq?(v1, v2)
  def eq?(%Just{}, %Nothing{}), do: false

  def not_eq?(%Just{value: v1}, %Just{value: v2}), do: not Eq.eq?(v1, v2)
  def not_eq?(%Just{}, %Nothing{}), do: true
end
```

- Just unwraps its value and defers comparison to the underlying Eq implementation.
- Just is never equal to Nothing.

lib/fun_park/monad/maybe/nothing.ex
```elixir
defimpl FunPark.Eq, for: FunPark.Monad.Maybe.Nothing do
  alias FunPark.Monad.Maybe.{Nothing, Just}

  def eq?(%Nothing{}, %Nothing{}), do: true
  def eq?(%Nothing{}, %Just{}), do: false

  def not_eq?(%Nothing{}, %Nothing{}), do: false
  def not_eq?(%Nothing{}, %Just{}), do: true
end
```

- Nothing is always equal to Nothing.
- Nothing is never equal to Just.

Because this Eq operates within the Maybe context, it must account for that quantum state; it needs one set of rules for *presence* and another for *absence*.

## Run It

Let's return to our Patron context, creating two versions of Alice—the original and a copy after she's updated her ticket to VIP:

```elixir
iex> alice = FunPark.Patron.make("Alice", 15, 150)
iex> alice_copy = FunPark.Patron.change(alice, %{ticket_tier: :vip})
```

Our Eq correctly recognizes that both records are still Alice—changing her ticket tier doesn't make Alice a different patron:

```elixir
iex> FunPark.Eq.Utils.eq?(alice, alice_copy)
true
```

And like the Identity monad, lifting both versions into the MaybePatron preserves the equality:

```elixir
iex> alice_maybe = FunPark.Monad.Maybe.pure(alice)
iex> alice_copy_maybe = FunPark.Monad.Maybe.pure(alice_copy)

iex> FunPark.Eq.Utils.eq?(alice_maybe, alice_copy_maybe)
true
```

However, refining the context to MaybeVipPatron draws a meaningful distinction between alice, who is *nothing* in this context, and alice_copy, who is *just* a VipPatron:

```elixir
iex> alice_maybe_vip = FunPark.Monad.Maybe.lift_predicate(
  alice, &FunPark.Patron.vip?/1
)
iex> alice_copy_maybe_vip = FunPark.Monad.Maybe.lift_predicate(
  alice_copy, &FunPark.Patron.vip?/1
)
```

Within the context of MaybeVipPatron, these two records are not equal:

```
iex> FunPark.Eq.Utils.eq?(alice_maybe_vip, alice_copy_maybe_vip)
false
```

Because within the refined context of MaybeVipPatron, the original Alice record is *nothing*.

## Establish Order

The Maybe context preserves the order of the underlying values while distinguishing between presence and absence.

Like Eq, to implement Ord in the context of Maybe, we must define order for each structure:

lib/fun_park/monad/maybe/just.ex
```
defimpl FunPark.Ord, for: FunPark.Monad.Maybe.Just do
  alias FunPark.Monad.Maybe.{Just, Nothing}
  alias FunPark.Ord

  def lt?(%Just{value: v1}, %Just{value: v2}), do: Ord.lt?(v1, v2)
  def lt?(%Just{}, %Nothing{}), do: false

  def le?(%Just{value: v1}, %Just{value: v2}), do: Ord.le?(v1, v2)
  def le?(%Just{}, %Nothing{}), do: false

  def gt?(%Just{value: v1}, %Just{value: v2}), do: Ord.gt?(v1, v2)
  def gt?(%Just{}, %Nothing{}), do: true

  def ge?(%Just{value: v1}, %Just{value: v2}), do: Ord.ge?(v1, v2)
  def ge?(%Just{}, %Nothing{}), do: true
end
```

- Just unwraps its value and defers comparison to the underlying Ord implementation.
- Just is always greater than Nothing.

lib/fun_park/monad/maybe/nothing.ex
```
defimpl FunPark.Ord, for: FunPark.Monad.Maybe.Nothing do
  alias FunPark.Monad.Maybe.{Nothing, Just}

  def lt?(%Nothing{}, %Just{}), do: true
  def lt?(%Nothing{}, %Nothing{}), do: false

  def le?(%Nothing{}, %Just{}), do: true
  def le?(%Nothing{}, %Nothing{}), do: true

  def gt?(%Nothing{}, %Just{}), do: false
  def gt?(%Nothing{}, %Nothing{}), do: false

  def ge?(%Nothing{}, %Just{}), do: false
  def ge?(%Nothing{}, %Nothing{}), do: true
end
```

- Nothing is always equal to Nothing.
- Nothing is always less than Just.

### Run It

Let's start by regenerating Alice and Beth:

```
iex> alice = FunPark.Patron.make("Alice", 15, 150, ticket_tier: :vip)
iex> beth = FunPark.Patron.make("Beth", 15, 150)
```

The default order for a Patron is alphabetical by name, so Alice is less than Beth:

```
iex> FunPark.Ord.Utils.compare(alice, beth)
:lt
```

And like Eq, lifting the patrons into MaybePatron preserves that order:

```
iex> alice_m = FunPark.Monad.Maybe.pure(alice)
iex> beth_m = FunPark.Monad.Maybe.pure(beth)

iex> FunPark.Ord.Utils.compare(alice_m, beth_m)
:lt
```

Also like Eq, refining the context to MaybeVipPatron changes the behavior:

```
iex> alice_vip =
FunPark.Monad.Maybe.lift_predicate(alice, &FunPark.Patron.vip?/1)

iex> beth_vip =
FunPark.Monad.Maybe.lift_predicate(beth, &FunPark.Patron.vip?/1)

iex> FunPark.Ord.Utils.compare(alice_vip, beth_vip)
:gt
```

Now, even though Beth's name comes after Alice alphabetically, the MaybeVip-Patron context treats Alice, with her VIP ticket, as greater than Beth—not because of any special ordering for VIPs but because in this refined context, Beth doesn't exist at all.

## Lift Custom Comparisons

Like the Identity monad, Maybe preserves the default Eq and Ord behavior. But as with Identity, custom comparisons must be explicitly lifted into the Maybe context.

We apply the custom equality only when both values are Just. All other combinations fall back to the default Maybe logic. (Code on next page.)

lib/fun_park/monad/maybe.ex
```elixir
def lift_eq(custom_eq) do
  custom_eq = Eq.Utils.to_eq_map(custom_eq)
  %{
    eq?: fn
      %Just{value: v1}, %Just{value: v2} -> custom_eq.eq?.(v1, v2)
      %Nothing{}, %Nothing{} -> true
      %Nothing{}, %Just{} -> false
      %Just{}, %Nothing{} -> false
    end,
    not_eq?: fn
      %Just{value: v1}, %Just{value: v2} -> custom_eq.not_eq?.(v1, v2)
      %Nothing{}, %Nothing{} -> false
      %Nothing{}, %Just{} -> true
      %Just{}, %Nothing{} -> true
    end
  }
end
```

As with Eq, the Ord custom logic applies only to Just values; other combinations respect the default ordering of the Maybe context.

```elixir
def lift_ord(custom_ord) do
  custom_ord = Ord.Utils.to_ord_map(custom_ord)
  %{
    lt?: fn
      %Just{value: v1}, %Just{value: v2} -> custom_ord.lt?.(v1, v2)
      %Nothing{}, %Nothing{} -> false
      %Nothing{}, %Just{} -> true
      %Just{}, %Nothing{} -> false
    end,
    le?: fn
      %Just{value: v1}, %Just{value: v2} -> custom_ord.le?.(v1, v2)
      %Nothing{}, %Nothing{} -> true
      %Nothing{}, %Just{} -> true
      %Just{}, %Nothing{} -> false
    end,
    gt?: fn
      %Just{value: v1}, %Just{value: v2} -> custom_ord.gt?.(v1, v2)
      %Nothing{}, %Nothing{} -> false
      %Just{}, %Nothing{} -> true
      %Nothing{}, %Just{} -> false
    end,
    ge?: fn
      %Just{value: v1}, %Just{value: v2} -> custom_ord.ge?.(v1, v2)
      %Nothing{}, %Nothing{} -> true
      %Just{}, %Nothing{} -> true
      %Nothing{}, %Just{} -> false
    end
  }
end
```

### Run It

Let's return to Alice and Beth:

```
iex> alice = FunPark.Patron.make("Alice", 15, 150, ticket_tier: :vip)
iex> beth = FunPark.Patron.make("Beth", 15, 150)
```

We'll compare patrons using ord_by_ticket_tier/0, where Alice, as a VIP, ranks higher than Beth:

```
iex> ord_by_ticket = FunPark.Patron.ord_by_ticket_tier()
iex> FunPark.Ord.Utils.compare(alice, beth, ord_by_ticket)
:gt
```

Now, let's lift both patrons into the Maybe context:

```
iex> alice_maybe = FunPark.Monad.Maybe.pure(alice)
iex> beth_maybe = FunPark.Monad.Maybe.pure(beth)
```

To use the same custom logic, we also need to lift the comparator:

```
iex> lifted_ord = FunPark.Monad.Maybe.lift_ord(ord_by_ticket)
```

Alice, with her VIP ticket, is greater:

```
iex> FunPark.Ord.Utils.compare(alice_maybe, beth_maybe, lifted_ord)
:gt
```

Here, we solved the VIP sorting problem in two ways: lift the vip?/1 predicate to refine the context, or lift a custom Ord to prioritize VIPs. If acting on a non-VIP would be invalid, lift the predicate and remove them from the context. If we need all patrons but just want to sort VIPs as higher priority, lift the Ord.

## Model Absence in a Monoid

Maybe solves a common monoidal problem: providing a suitable context when the outcome needs to represent the possibility of absence.

- Nothing serves as the identity, explicitly representing the absence of a value.
- Just holds a result that combines according to the underlying monoid.

We left Prioritize a Patron, on page 63, with a priority queue that needs to include the possibility the queue might be empty.

Let's revisit Patron.max_priority_monoid/0 in the code on the next page:

```
lib/fun_park/patron.ex
defp max_priority_monoid do
  %Monoid.Max{
    value: priority_empty(),
    ord: ord_by_priority()
  }
end
```

Here, the caller has to infer that the synthetic patron returned by priority_empty/0 signals an empty queue. By wrapping the result in Maybe, we make that absence explicit—using structure to represent the possibility of no result.

```
lib/fun_park/patron.ex
def max_priority_maybe_monoid do
  %Monoid.Max{
    value: Maybe.nothing(),
    ord: Maybe.lift_ord(ord_by_priority())
  }
end
```

This changes the identity to Nothing and lifts the custom ordering into the Maybe context. The max monoid behaves the same, but now emptiness is expressed through structure rather than a sentinel value.

Finally, we update highest_priority/1, the function that applies our priority monoid, to lift its patrons into the MaybePatron context:

```
lib/fun_park/patron.ex
def highest_priority_maybe(patrons) when is_list(patrons) do
  m_concat(
    max_priority_maybe_monoid(),
    patrons |> Enum.map(&Maybe.pure/1)
  )
end
```

Structuring everything within Maybe removes the ambiguity: the result is always either *just* the highest-priority patron or *nothing*.

Here, we didn't rewrite the monoid—we just lifted everything into Maybe, allowing it to represent the *possibility* of a value.

## Run It

Start by creating three patrons:

```
iex> alice = FunPark.Patron.make(
  "Alice", 15, 120,
  reward_points: 50, ticket_tier: :premium
)

iex> beth = FunPark.Patron.make(
```

```
  "Beth", 16, 130,
  reward_points: 20, ticket_tier: :vip
)
iex> charles = FunPark.Patron.make(
  "Charles", 14, 135,
  reward_points: 150, ticket_tier: :premium
)
```

Using highest_priority_maybe/1, we determine who should go next:

```
iex> FunPark.Patron.highest_priority_maybe([alice, beth, charles])
%FunPark.Monad.Maybe.Just{
  value: %FunPark.Patron{name: "Beth", ...}
}
iex> FunPark.Patron.highest_priority_maybe([alice, charles])
%FunPark.Monad.Maybe.Just{
  value: %FunPark.Patron{name: "Charles", ...}
}
iex> FunPark.Patron.highest_priority_maybe([alice])
%FunPark.Monad.Maybe.Just{
  value: %FunPark.Patron{name: "Alice", ...}
}
```

And when the queue is empty, the result is *nothing*:

```
iex> FunPark.Patron.highest_priority_maybe([])
%FunPark.Monad.Maybe.Nothing{}
```

Rather than a sentinel, our highest_priority_maybe/1 returns a MaybePatron, where presence and absence are encoded in the structure itself.

## Implement the Monadic Behaviors

Maybe, like all monads, isn't closed under arbitrary operations—it's closed under its monadic interface. This means we can't simply pipe Maybe contexts together; we need to use map/2, bind/2, or ap/2, which are designed to apply functions while preserving the context.

To implement the Monad behavior for Maybe, we implement the protocol for Just and Nothing.

The protocol for Nothing is shown on the next page.

lib/fun_park/monad/maybe/nothing.ex
```elixir
defimpl FunPark.Monad, for: FunPark.Monad.Maybe.Nothing do
  alias FunPark.Monad.Maybe.Nothing

  def map(%Nothing{}, _func), do: %Nothing{}
  def ap(%Nothing{}, _val), do: %Nothing{}
  def bind(%Nothing{}, _func), do: %Nothing{}
end
```

All operations on Nothing return Nothing.

And here it is for Just:

lib/fun_park/monad/maybe/just.ex
```elixir
defimpl FunPark.Monad, for: FunPark.Monad.Maybe.Just do
  alias FunPark.Monad.Maybe.{Just, Nothing}

  def map(%Just{value: value}, func), do: Just.pure(func.(value))

  def ap(%Just{value: func}, %Just{value: value}),
    do: Just.pure(func.(value))

  def ap(%Just{}, %Nothing{}), do: %Nothing{}

  def bind(%Just{value: value}, func), do: func.(value)
end
```

- map/2 applies the transformation and wraps the result back in Just, preserving structure.
- ap/2 applies the wrapped function to the wrapped value if both are Just; otherwise, it returns Nothing.
- bind/2 applies a function that returns a Maybe, transforming the value and potentially changing structure.

## Functor Map

Our Ride expert has raised a new issue: wait times should only be updated for online rides.

To enforce this, we can use the online?/1 predicate to refine a Ride into MaybeOnlineRide:

```elixir
def update_wait_time_maybe(%__MODULE__{} = ride, wait_time)
    when is_number(wait_time) do
  ride
  |> Maybe.lift_predicate(&online?/1)
  |> map(&update_wait_time(&1, wait_time))
end
```

In the context of MaybeOnlineRide, map/2 applies update_wait_time/2 to an online ride.

## Run It

First, let's generate an offline Tea Cup ride:

```
iex> tea_cup = FunPark.Ride.make("Tea Cup", online: false)
iex> FunPark.Ride.update_wait_time_maybe(tea_cup, 20)
%FunPark.Monad.Maybe.Nothing{}
```

Within our MaybeOnlineRide context, the Tea Cup is *nothing*, so updating its wait time returns *nothing*.

Later, the ride comes back online:

```
iex> tea_cup = FunPark.Ride.change(tea_cup, %{online: true})
```

Now, Tea Cup is *just* an OnlineRide, so the transformation is applied.

```
iex> FunPark.Ride.update_wait_time_maybe(tea_cup, 20)
%FunPark.Monad.Maybe.Just{
  value: %FunPark.Ride{ name: "Tea Cup", wait_time: 20, online: true, ... }
}
```

Here, we're making illegal states unrepresentable: within the MaybeOnlineRide context, it's not possible to accidentally update the wait time of a ride that doesn't exist.

## Monad Bind

Previously with Fast Lane Access, on page 86, we used predicate composition to define fast lane eligibility. Let's update this logic: instead of just returning the rule, we'll use monadic composition, applying control flow and forwarding the patron.

First, we lift the predicate into the Maybe monad, creating a MaybeEligiblePatron.

lib/fun_park/ride.ex
```
def check_ride_eligibility(%Patron{} = patron, %__MODULE__{} = ride) do
  is_eligible = curry_r(&eligible?/2)
  Maybe.lift_predicate(patron, is_eligible.(ride))
end
```

Next, we do the same for a valid FastPass, producing a MaybePatronWithPass:

lib/fun_park/ride.ex
```
def check_fast_pass(%Patron{} = patron, %__MODULE__{} = ride) do
  has_fast_pass = curry_r(&fast_pass?/2)
  Maybe.lift_predicate(patron, has_fast_pass.(ride))
end
```

These are Kleisli functions—they take a value and return a Maybe. To compose them, we use bind/2:

```
def fast_pass_lane(%Patron{} = patron, %__MODULE__{} = ride) do
  check_fast_pass = curry_r(&check_fast_pass/2)

  patron
  |> check_ride_eligibility(ride)
  |> bind(check_fast_pass.(ride))
end
```

When we chain functions with bind/2, we progressively narrow the context—in this case, to a MaybeFastLanePatron.

So bind/2 doesn't just compose logic, it composes context. Each step adds a conjunctive constraint, evolving logic and context together. We implement our domain rules by limiting the context to valid scenarios, making the illegal unrepresentable.

## Run It

Let's start by setting up a Ride, a FastPass, and a couple of Patrons:

```
iex> haunted_mansion = FunPark.Ride.make("Haunted Mansion", min_age: 14)
iex> datetime = DateTime.new!(~D[2025-06-01], ~T[13:00:00])
iex> fast_pass = FunPark.FastPass.make(haunted_mansion, datetime)

iex> alice = FunPark.Patron.make("Alice", 15, 150)
iex> beth = FunPark.Patron.make("Beth", 13, 130)
```

Alice does not qualify for the fast lane:

```
iex> FunPark.Ride.fast_pass_lane(alice, haunted_mansion)
%FunPark.Monad.Maybe.Nothing{}
```

To qualify, we give her a FastPass:

```
iex> alice = FunPark.Patron.add_fast_pass(alice, fast_pass)

iex> FunPark.Ride.fast_pass_lane(alice, haunted_mansion)
%FunPark.Monad.Maybe.Just{
  value: %FunPark.Patron{ name: "Alice", ... }
}
```

Beth is too young for the Haunted Mansion, so even with a FastPass, she doesn't qualify:

```
iex> beth = FunPark.Patron.add_fast_pass(beth, fast_pass)

iex> FunPark.Ride.fast_pass_lane(beth, haunted_mansion)
%FunPark.Monad.Maybe.Nothing{}
```

## Recovery

Yikes! Our Ride expert reminds us that a VIP who is eligible for a ride doesn't need a FastPass. Right now, we're enforcing Ride eligibility *and* a FastPass, but we need to adjust the logic to allow either a FastPass *or* a VIP Patron.

The Maybe monad is biased toward Just—it's conjunctive, with each bind/2 adding a condition that must succeed. But this problem is disjunctive, so we need a way to recover when one path fails—in this case, a logical fallback with or_else/2.

lib/fun_park/monad/maybe.ex
```
def or_else(%Nothing{}, fallback_fun) when is_function(fallback_fun, 0),
  do: fallback_fun.()

def or_else(%Just{} = just, _fallback_fun), do: just
```

Here, if the structure is Just, it remains unchanged. If Nothing, it calls the fallback thunk.

We can use or_else/2 to implement our or VIP logic:

lib/fun_park/ride.ex
```
def check_vip_or_fast_pass(patron, ride) do
  is_vip = &Patron.vip?/1

  patron
  |> Maybe.lift_predicate(is_vip)
  |> Maybe.or_else(fn -> check_fast_pass(patron, ride) end)
end
```

• If the patron is a VIP, they qualify immediately.
• If not, it falls back to checking whether they have a valid FastPass.

Notice that we're not collapsing the structure (folding). We're still in the quantum *possibility* of a value, but now it includes VIP patrons.

Finally, we can update check_ride_eligibility/2 to operate within the MaybeFastLane-Patron context.

lib/fun_park/ride.ex
```
def fast_pass_lane(%Patron{} = patron, %__MODULE__{} = ride) do
  check_vip_or_pass = curry_r(&check_vip_or_fast_pass/2)

  patron
  |> check_ride_eligibility(ride)
  |> bind(check_vip_or_pass.(ride))
end
```

> Once you start to internalize mental maps, you'll notice there are often multiple ways to reach the same result. In this case, we could have handled all of the predicate logic first, then lifted it into the Maybe monad.

## Run It

Let's generate Charles:

```
iex> charles = FunPark.Patron.make("Charles", 15, 145)
```

Although Charles is eligible for the Haunted Mansion, he has neither a Fast-Pass nor a VIP; he is *nothing* in our MaybeFastLanePatron context.

```
iex> FunPark.Ride.fast_pass_lane(charles, haunted_mansion)
%FunPark.Monad.Maybe.Nothing{}
```

Later, he upgrades to VIP:

```
iex> charles = FunPark.Patron.change(charles, %{ticket_tier: :vip})
```

And now he qualifies:

```
iex> FunPark.Ride.fast_pass_lane(charles, haunted_mansion)
%FunPark.Monad.Maybe.Just{
  value: %FunPark.Patron{ name: "Charles", ticket_tier: :vip, ... }
}
```

Charles, with his VIP pass, is now a member of the FastLanePatron context.

# Refine Lists

Our Ride expert points out a new challenge: patrons often arrive as families or groups, so we need to treat them as collections of patrons, not just individuals.

## Concat

In the fast lane, we include only those who qualify. We need to reduce a list of MaybeFastLanePatron to a list of FastLanePatron. This operation is often called flatten, compact, or collect. In Haskell, it's called catMaybes, so we'll call ours Maybe.concat.

lib/fun_park/monad/maybe.ex
```
def concat(list) when is_list(list) do
  list
  |> fold_l([], fn
    %Just{value: value}, acc -> [value | acc]
    %Nothing{}, acc -> acc
  end)
  |> :lists.reverse()
end
```

Here, concat/2 uses fold_l/3 to collect *just* values, discarding *nothing*. Because Elixir uses linked lists, we prepend during reduction and reverse the result to preserve the original order.

We can use concat/1 to solve our group problem:

lib/fun_park/ride.ex
```
def only_fast_pass_lane_concat(patrons, %__MODULE__{} = ride)
    when is_list(patrons) do
  patrons
  |> Enum.map(&fast_pass_lane(&1, ride))
  |> Maybe.concat()
end
```

Our Kleisli function, fast_pass_lane/2, takes a value and returns a Maybe. We use Enum.map/2 to turn a list of Patron into a list of MaybeFastLanePatron, then call Maybe.concat/1 to collapse that into a list of FastLanePatron.

## Run It

Let's start by generating a Ride, a FastPass, and some Patrons:

```
iex> haunted_mansion = FunPark.Ride.make("Haunted Mansion", min_age: 14)
iex> datetime = DateTime.new!(~D[2025-06-01], ~T[13:00:00])
iex> fast_pass = FunPark.FastPass.make(haunted_mansion, datetime)

iex> alice = FunPark.Patron.make("Alice", 15, 150)
iex> beth = FunPark.Patron.make("Beth", 13, 135)
iex> charles = FunPark.Patron.make("Charles", 15, 145)
```

Next, we'll give Alice and Beth FastPasses, and upgrade Charles to VIP:

```
iex> alice = FunPark.Patron.add_fast_pass(alice, fast_pass)
iex> beth = FunPark.Patron.add_fast_pass(beth, fast_pass)
iex> charles = FunPark.Patron.change(charles, %{ticket_tier: :vip})
```

Now, we can use only_fast_pass_lane/2 to refine our list of Patron to a list of Fast-LanePatron, as shown on the next page.

```
iex> patrons = [alice, beth, charles]
```

```
iex> FunPark.Ride.only_fast_pass_lane_concat(patrons, haunted_mansion)
[
  %FunPark.Patron{ name: "Alice", ... },
  %FunPark.Patron{ name: "Charles", ... }
]
```

The result includes Alice and Charles. Although Beth holds a valid FastPass, she's too young for the Haunted Mansion and is excluded.

But while only_fast_pass_lane/2 works, it introduces an extra Enum.map/2 loop.

## Concat Map

In only_fast_pass_lane_concat/2, we used Enum.map/2 with a Kleisli function to lift each Patron into the Maybe context—looping once to wrap the data and again to discard the Nothing values. But we can do both in a single pass using concat_map/2, which accepts a Kleisli function and collapses the results as it goes.

lib/fun_park/monad/maybe.ex
```
def concat_map(list, func) when is_list(list) and is_function(func, 1) do
  fold_l(list, [], fn item, acc ->
    case func.(item) do
      %Just{value: value} -> [value | acc]
      %Nothing{} -> acc
    end
  end)
  |> :lists.reverse()
end
```

With concat_map/2, we get the same behavior but without the extra loop:

lib/fun_park/ride.ex
```
def only_fast_pass_lane(patrons, %__MODULE__{} = ride)
    when is_list(patrons) do
  patrons
  |> Maybe.concat_map(&fast_pass_lane(&1, ride))
end
```

## Run It

Let's return to our patrons and ride. The only_fast_pass_lane/2 function still returns *just* the eligible patrons:

```
iex> patrons = [alice, beth, charles]
iex> FunPark.Ride.only_fast_pass_lane(patrons, haunted_mansion)
[
  %FunPark.Patron{ name: "Alice", ... },
  %FunPark.Patron{ name: "Charles", ... }
]
```

We get the same results but without the extra loop.

## Sequence

Although pleased with our progress, our Ride expert points out that we didn't quite get this right. Groups don't want to be split up. We don't need a list of eligible patrons; we need *just* the FastLanePatronGroup, or *nothing*.

More specifically, we need a *sequence*, a term from category theory describing the transformation of a list of effects into an effect of a list. In the context of Maybe, sequence returns *just* the full list if every element is Just, or *nothing* if any element is Nothing.

```
lib/fun_park/monad/maybe.ex
def sequence([]), do: pure([])

def sequence([head | tail]) do
  bind(head, fn value ->
    bind(sequence(tail), fn rest ->
      pure([value | rest])
    end)
  end)
end
```

Because the Maybe monad is *just*-biased, the base case returns *just* an empty list. For non-empty lists, we use bind/2 to process each element and recursively call sequence/1, returning *just* the collected values—or short-circuiting to *nothing* if any element is *nothing*.

With sequence/1, we can solve the group issue:

```
def group_fast_pass_lane(patrons, %__MODULE__{} = ride)
    when is_list(patrons) do
  patrons
  |> Enum.map(&fast_pass_lane(&1, ride))
  |> Maybe.sequence()
end
```

Here, we map a list of Patron to MaybeFastLanePatron, then use sequence/1 to produce *just* a FastLanePatronGroup or *nothing*.

## Run It

Let's reuse our Ride and Patrons:

Remember, even though she has a FastPass, Beth is too young, so the group cannot enter the fast lane:

```
iex> patrons = [alice, beth, charles]
iex> FunPark.Ride.group_fast_pass_lane(patrons, haunted_mansion)
%FunPark.Monad.Maybe.Nothing{}
```

However, if Beth steps aside, as a group Alice and Charles can enter the fast lane:

```
iex> FunPark.Ride.group_fast_pass_lane([alice, charles], haunted_mansion)
%FunPark.Monad.Maybe.Just{
  value: [
    %FunPark.Patron{ name: "Alice", ...},
    %FunPark.Patron{ name: "Charles", ... }
  ]
}
```

## Not So Fast

If we take a closer look at our logic, we'll see a subtle problem:

```
def group_fast_pass_lane(patrons, %__MODULE__{} = ride)
    when is_list(patrons) do
  patrons
  |> Enum.map(&fast_pass_lane(&1, ride))
  |> Maybe.sequence()
end
```

While both fast_pass_lane/2 and sequence/1 support short-circuiting on *nothing*, Elixir's Enum.map/2 is eager—it evaluates the entire list before sequence/1 is ever called. So even if Beth fails the check, Charles is still evaluated, wasting work.

To short-circuit as early as possible, we need to avoid the eager Enum.map/2 with a *traverse*.

## Traverse

Our group_fast_pass_lane/2 maps and then sequences, which is a naive traverse. Let's start with that pattern:

```
def traverse(list, func) when is_list(list) do
  list
  |> Enum.map(func)
  |> sequence()
end
```

Again, the logic is correct, but Elixir's eager evaluation in Enum.map/2 runs the function on every element, even if one fails early. We can do better by short-circuiting, just like we did in sequence/2:

```
def traverse([], _func), do: pure([])
def traverse([head | tail], func) do
  bind(func.(head), fn value ->
    bind(traverse(tail, func), fn rest ->
      pure([value | rest])
    end)
  end)
end
```

Here, the base case is *just* an empty list. As soon as the Kleisli function (func) returns *nothing*, bind/2 halts the traversal, skipping any unnecessary work.

### Not Quite

We can do even better. This recursive implementation risks a stack overflow with very large lists. Elixir, like many functional languages, supports *tail recursion*—an optimization that reuses the current function's stack frame to avoid growing the call stack.

But while we could refactor our code for tail recursion, there's a better option: Elixir's Enum.reduce_while/3 already includes this optimization and supports short-circuiting, making it safe for large lists.

lib/fun_park/monad/maybe.ex
```
def traverse([], _func), do: pure([])
def traverse(list, func) when is_list(list) and is_function(func, 1) do
  list
  |> Enum.reduce_while(pure([]), fn item, %Just{value: acc} ->
    case func.(item) do
      %Just{value: value} -> {:cont, pure([value | acc])}
      %Nothing{} -> {:halt, nothing()}
    end
  end)
  |> map(&:lists.reverse/1)
end
```

Here, reduce_while/3 enables early termination when func.(item) returns *nothing*, ensuring no unnecessary computations are performed. The accumulator collects values in reverse order for efficiency, and map/2 applies Erlang's :lists/reverse/1, restoring the original order.

Now we can update group_fast_pass_lane/2:

lib/fun_park/ride.ex
```
def group_fast_pass_lane(patrons, %__MODULE__{} = ride)
    when is_list(patrons) do
  Maybe.traverse(patrons, &fast_pass_lane(&1, ride))
end
```

This produces the same result but short-circuits as soon as any patron fails the fast-lane check.

We started by thinking that traverse/2 implemented sequence/1, but it's more accurate to say that sequence/1 is a special case of traverse/2—using the identity function as the transformer.

```
def sequence(list) when is_list(list), do: traverse(list, fn x -> x end)
```

### Run It

Returning to our patrons and ride, we get the same results—Beth is too young for the Haunted Mansion. But with traverse/2, the process short-circuits as soon as an ineligible patron is found. Beth's age fails the check, halting evaluation before Charles is even considered:

```
iex patrons = [alice, beth, charles]
iex> FunPark.Ride.group_fast_pass_lane(patrons, haunted_mansion)
%FunPark.Monad.Maybe.Nothing{}
```

As we saw in this section, Maybe isn't limited to refining single values—it can refine collections. Whether we're filtering for those who belong or ensuring that everyone does, Maybe gives us a way to express presence and absence across a group.

### Act on It

We've defined a priority queue for our patrons and logic to determine whether a patron can use the FastPass lane. Now, our Ride expert wants to combine that logic, creating a priority queue for each ride's fast lane.

This is a max monoid problem, but instead of working within the broader MaybePatron context, apply the queue inside the more refined MaybeFastPassPatron context.

Find the Maybe Chapter Answers, on page 214.

## Filter Within Composition

When we think of filtering, our first instinct is probably removing items from a list. But Filterable is more general: it's about conditionally retaining or discarding values in any context. For a list, that means removing elements that don't meet a condition; for Maybe, it means keeping *just* the value if the condition holds.

Filterable can be implemented as a protocol:

```
lib/fun_park/filterable.ex
defprotocol FunPark.Filterable do
  def guard(structure, bool)
  def filter(structure, predicate)
  def filter_map(structure, func)
end
```

- guard/2 retains the value if the Boolean is true and discards it otherwise.
- filter/2 retains the value if the predicate passes.
- filter_map/2 applies a transformation that may also discard the value.

Next, we implement the Filterable protocol for Maybe.

Since Nothing holds no value, there's no evaluation to perform and each operation returns Nothing.

```
lib/fun_park/monad/maybe/nothing.ex
defimpl FunPark.Filterable, for: FunPark.Monad.Maybe.Nothing do
  alias FunPark.Monad.Maybe.Nothing

  def guard(%Nothing{}, _boolean), do: %Nothing{}
  def filter(%Nothing{}, _predicate), do: %Nothing{}
  def filter_map(%Nothing{}, _func), do: %Nothing{}
end
```

And we need logic for Just:

```
lib/fun_park/monad/maybe/just.ex
defimpl FunPark.Filterable, for: FunPark.Monad.Maybe.Just do
  alias FunPark.Monad.Maybe
  alias FunPark.Monad.Maybe.Just
  alias FunPark.Monad

  def guard(%Just{} = maybe, true), do: maybe
  def guard(%Just{}, false), do: Maybe.nothing()

  def filter(%Just{} = maybe, predicate) do
    Monad.bind(maybe, fn value ->
      if predicate.(value) do
        Maybe.pure(value)
      else
        Maybe.nothing()
      end
    end)
  end

  def filter_map(%Just{value: value}, func) do
    case func.(value) do
      %Just{} = just -> just
      _ -> Maybe.nothing()
    end
  end
end
```

- guard/2 retains the original Just if the condition is true; otherwise, it returns Nothing.
- filter/2 applies a predicate to the contained value. If the predicate returns true, it keeps the value in a Just; if not, it returns Nothing.
- filter_map/2 applies a transformation that returns a Maybe. If the result is a Just, it's returned; otherwise, it returns Nothing.

## Guard

Earlier, our Ride expert pointed out that we can only update the wait time in the OnlineRide context—but there's another rule: wait times can't be negative. We can handle this by adding a guard/2 in our pipeline:

```
lib/fun_park/ride.ex
def update_wait_time_maybe(%__MODULE__{} = ride, wait_time)
    when is_number(wait_time) do
  ride
  |> Maybe.lift_predicate(&online?/1)
  |> guard(wait_time >= 0)
  |> map(&update_wait_time(&1, wait_time))
end
```

This updates the wait time for *just* an OnlineRide—but only if the wait time is valid.

We could check at the function head with when is_number(wait_time) and wait_time >= 0, but that would raise an error if the condition fails. Using Maybe keeps the check inside the context, returning Nothing instead of crashing on invalid input.

Where you place the guard depends on what the caller is expected to know. Here, we assume the caller can provide a number but may not have the context to judge whether it's valid.

## Run It

Let's start by generating a ride:

```
iex> tea_cup = FunPark.Ride.make("Tea Cup")
```

Update with a positive number and we get *just* the ride:

```
iex> FunPark.Ride.update_wait_time_maybe(tea_cup, 10)
%FunPark.Monad.Maybe.Just{
  value: %FunPark.Ride{ name: "Tea Cup", wait_time: 10, ... }
}
```

But if we provide a negative number, the guard short-circuits:

```
iex> FunPark.Ride.update_wait_time_maybe(tea_cup, -10)
%FunPark.Monad.Maybe.Nothing{}
```

The pipeline continues to respect the OnlineRide context. If we update the Tea Cup to be offline, it returns *nothing*, even with a valid wait time:

```
iex> tea_cup = FunPark.Ride.change(tea_cup, %{online: false})

iex> FunPark.Ride.update_wait_time_maybe(tea_cup, 10)
%FunPark.Monad.Maybe.Nothing{}
```

## Filter

Our Patron expert has a new concern: patrons are frustrated when they add a FastPass only to later discover they're not eligible to ride. To prevent this, we should only allow patrons to add a FastPass when they meet the ride's eligibility requirements.

We have two options: we can refine the context to an EligiblePatron using lift_predicate/2 or apply the check within the current context using filter/2. The difference is semantic—what matters is which approach best reflects how Patron experts reason about eligibility.

```
lib/fun_park/patron.ex
def add_fast_pass_maybe(%__MODULE__{} = patron, fast_pass) do
  ride = FastPass.get_ride(fast_pass)
  new_passes = List.union([fast_pass], get_fast_passes(patron))
  update_fast_pass = Utils.curry_r(&change/2)
  eligible = Utils.curry_r(&Ride.eligible?/2)

  patron
  |> Maybe.pure()
  |> filter(eligible.(ride))
  |> map(update_fast_pass.(%{fast_passes: new_passes}))
end
```

This wraps the Patron in a Maybe, checks eligibility with filter/2, and if eligible, updates their fast_passes with map/2. It short-circuits to Nothing if the Patron doesn't qualify.

Both lift_predicate/2 and filter/2 serve similar purposes. The difference is perspective: Are we refining the context or applying a condition within the existing one?

### FilterMap

Both `bind/2` and `filter_map/2` produce the same result. Again, we choose based on intent.

If our `Ride` expert describes `check_ride_eligibility/2` and `check_vip_or_pass/1` as a sequence of dependent steps—where each step must succeed before the next—then we use `bind/2` to emphasize that chain of dependency:

```
lib/fun_park/ride.ex
def fast_pass_lane(%Patron{} = patron, %__MODULE__{} = ride) do
  check_vip_or_pass = curry_r(&check_vip_or_fast_pass/2)

  patron
  |> check_ride_eligibility(ride)
  |> bind(check_vip_or_pass.(ride))
end
```

But if the logic is framed as "first check this, then continue if it passes," we use `filter_map/2`, highlighting the conditional gating rather than dependency:

```
def fast_pass_lane(%Patron{} = patron, %__MODULE__{} = ride) do
  check_vip_or_pass = curry_r(&check_vip_or_fast_pass/2).(ride)

  patron
  |> check_ride_eligibility(ride)
  |> filter_map(check_vip_or_pass)
end
```

Our goal is to reflect domain logic clearly, reinforcing the ubiquitous language shared between developers and domain experts.

## What You've Learned

The `Maybe` monad gives us a structured way to model the *possibility* of a value. Instead of relying on ad-hoc `nil` checks, we make uncertainty explicit—Just for presence, `Nothing` for absence.

Monadic functions let us build pipelines that stay within the context of absence. `map/2` transforms while preserving structure; `bind/2` sequences conditionally, continuing only when a value is present. `Maybe` also integrates with lists through operations like `sequence`, `traverse`, and `concat`, allowing uncertainty to flow through collections in a controlled, predictable way. And because `Maybe` can contain a value, it supports comparison and ordering.

Sprinkling in defensive code is quick and familiar: a guard here, a default there—each patch feels small, local, and easy to justify. For teams focused on closing tickets, it's often the path of least resistance. But over time, scattered checks blur intent and quietly duplicate logic. `Maybe` asks for more up front: it invites us to model absence as part of the domain—replacing patches with structure and trading short-term convenience for long-term clarity.

And in domains that evolve, Maybe grows with your understanding. It captures partial knowledge, enforces structure, and keeps logic explicit—turning uncertainty into something you can model, compose, and build on.

In the next chapter, we'll look at Either, a monad that extends the branching behavior of Maybe. In the Maybe context, we distinguish between something and nothing. The Either context adds detail to the "nothing" side, carrying information about *why* a computation failed.

> Does this chapter feel impossible? That's feedback, *not* failure. Meaningful learning requires repetition. Go back and revisit earlier chapters—dig into the fuzzy parts; poke at what doesn't quite click. You need these structures in your long-term memory to be able to reuse them in a new context.

# CHAPTER 9

# Model Outcomes with Either

A production-ready Either is available in the Funx library.[1]

You're booking a flight and receive a message:

- Name field cannot be blank.
- Return date must be after departure date.
- Phone number is invalid.

The system has established a boundary, protecting itself from your invalid input but giving a path forward.

This is an Either: the system defends itself but returns *why* it failed.

Once you internalize the idea of context-aware failure, Either starts showing up everywhere. It goes beyond form validation to access control, audit trails, and business rules—decisions that must be explained, not just detected.

While Maybe captures the *possibility* of a value, Either represents the *possibility* of success. They share a branching structure, but Either adds information to the failure path.

We won't retread what you learned in Maybe. Instead, we'll build on that foundation—using Either to handle complex validation and, later, to bring structure to native error-handling.

But first, let's begin with the core: how Either is structured.

---

1.   https://hexdocs.pm/funx/Funx.Monad.Either.html

# Structure of Either

Either represents branching logic using Right and Left. Unlike Maybe, both variants carry a value—one for success, one for failure.

lib/fun_park/monad/either/right.ex
```
defmodule FunPark.Monad.Either.Right do
  @enforce_keys [:right]
  defstruct [:right]

  def pure(value), do: %__MODULE__{right: value}
end
```

lib/fun_park/monad/either/left.ex
```
defmodule FunPark.Monad.Either.Left do
  @enforce_keys [:left]
  defstruct [:left]

  def pure(value), do: %__MODULE__{left: value}
end
```

Together, they define the Either context: a structure that behaves like Maybe but says more.

## Eq

Equality in the Either context depends on both the branch and the contents. Two Right values are equal if their inner values are equal. Two Left values are equal if their inner values are equal. A Right is never equal to a Left, even if they contain the same value.

## Ord

Ordering follows the same logic. When both sides are the same variant, their contents are compared using the Ord protocol. But a Left is always considered less than a Right, regardless of their inner values.

## Foldable

Like Maybe, Either can be folded. Folding collapses the binary structure to a single result. Either also includes get_or_else/2 and filter_or_else/3, which leverage fold.

## Filterable

Here's where Either diverges from Maybe. While Maybe can be filtered freely, Either can't generate a new Left when a predicate fails. It's not possible to construct an error from nothing.

## Monad

The Either context supports monadic composition through map/2, bind/2, and ap/2. These work exactly as they do in Maybe, with Left taking the place of Nothing.

- map/2 transforms the Right value, leaving Left untouched.
- bind/2 sequences computations that may fail, propagating the first Left encountered.
- ap/2 applies a Right(function) to a Right(value); if either is a Left, the failure short-circuits.

This structure allows computation to continue as long as things succeed, while making failure immediate and explicit.

As with all branching monads, Either has a bias. It favors the success path: Right represents success, and Left represents failure. This bias is what allows map, bind, and ap to compose along the Right branch and short-circuit on Left.

## Either Module

The Either module provides functions for constructing, inspecting, and adapting Either values. These mirror those in Maybe but are adapted for cases where both branches carry data.

We construct values using right/1, left/1, or the more general pure/1. We can check which branch we're working with using right?/1 and left?/1.

Like Maybe, Either supports lifting. We can bring behavior into the structure with functions like lift_maybe/2, lift_predicate/3, lift_eq/1, and lift_ord/1. We can also interoperate with native Elixir using from_result/1, to_result/1, from_try/1, and to_try!/1.

Now that you understand how Either is structured, let's move on to real-world problems.

# Validation

Our Ride expert reports that patrons are frustrated when they're excluded from the fast lane. While our current logic prevents ineligible patrons from entering, it doesn't explain *why* they were denied.

## Ride Eligibility

To address this, we'll switch context from Maybe to Either, where we have either Right(eligible_patron) or Left(reason_for_denial).

We already have the predicates; we just need to lift them into an Either.

```
lib/fun_park/monad/either.ex
def lift_predicate(value, predicate, on_false)
    when is_function(predicate, 1) and is_function(on_false, 1) do
  fold_l(
    fn -> predicate.(value) end,
    fn -> right(value) end,
    fn -> left(on_false.(value)) end
  )
end
```

The lift_predicate/3 function for Either is similar to the one in Maybe but adds a
thunked callback to generate the Left value. This callback receives the original
input, giving it context about what failed, and is only evaluated if the predicate
does not pass.

Our Ride module is getting overloaded, so let's introduce a FastLane service to
hold the eligibility rules. In *Domain-Driven Design [Eva03]*, a service is a logical
grouping of operations that don't naturally belong to a single entity.

In object-oriented programming, services are typically defined as pure functions without mutation or side effects. In functional programming—where
functions are already pure—services serve a different role: they're an organi-
zational tool, grouping related behavior under a shared namespace.

First, let's ensure the height requirement within our new FastLane service:

```
lib/fun_park/ride/fast_lane.ex
def ensure_height(%Patron{} = patron, %Ride{} = ride) do
  patron
  |> Either.lift_predicate(
    curry_r(&Ride.tall_enough?/2).(ride),
    fn p -> "#{Patron.get_name(p)} is not tall enough" end
  )
  |> Either.map_left(&ValidationError.new/1)
end
```

Here, ensure_height/2 is a Kleisli function: it takes a Patron and returns an Either
monad using our tall_enough?/2 predicate.

On failure, it returns a context-specific error wrapped in a ValidationError,
allowing downstream callers to distinguish validation issues from other errors.

Next, we ensure the age requirement:

```
lib/fun_park/ride/fast_lane.ex
def ensure_age(%Patron{} = patron, %Ride{} = ride) do
  patron
  |> Either.lift_predicate(
    curry_r(&Ride.old_enough?/2).(ride),
    fn p -> "#{Patron.get_name(p)} is not old enough" end
```

```
  )
  |> Either.map_left(&ValidationError.new/1)
end
```

This is also Kleisli function, taking a Patron and returning Either Right(Patron) or Left(ValidationError), but this time checking the patron's age.

Let's take a closer look at our ValidationError:

lib/fun_park/errors/validation_error.ex
```
defmodule FunPark.Errors.ValidationError do
  defstruct errors: [], __exception__: true

  @behaviour Exception

  def new(errors) when is_list(errors), do: %__MODULE__{errors: errors}

  def new(error), do: %__MODULE__{errors: [error]}

  def merge(%__MODULE__{errors: e1}, %__MODULE__{errors: e2}),
    do: %__MODULE__{errors: e1 ++ e2}

  @impl Exception
  def exception(args) when is_list(args), do: struct(__MODULE__, args)

  @impl Exception
  def exception(message) when is_binary(message),
    do: %__MODULE__{errors: [message]}

  @impl Exception
  def message(%__MODULE__{errors: errors}) do
    Enum.map_join(errors, ", ", &to_string/1)
  end
end
```

ValidationError models one or more validation issues as a structured exception. It holds a list of error messages and provides two core operations:

- new/1: Wraps a single message or a list of messages.
- merge/2: Combines two structs by joining their message lists.

Since Elixir has no built-in validation error type, we define our own by implementing the Exception behavior. As *Programming Elixir [Tho18]* notes, exceptions in Elixir are just structs that implement the Exception protocol:

- exception/1: Builds the struct from a keyword list or a single string.
- message/1: Returns a formatted string by joining the error messages.

We also set _exception_: true in the struct so that Elixir recognizes it as an exception at compile time.

## Run it

Start Elixir's iex shell and run the mix script to compile the code and load the project.

```
iex -S mix
```

Let's start by generating a couple of patrons and a ride:

```
iex> alice = FunPark.Patron.make("Alice", 12, 125, ticket_tier: :vip)
iex> beth = FunPark.Patron.make("Beth", 16, 115)
iex> haunted_mansion = FunPark.Ride.make(
  "Haunted Mansion",
  min_age: 14,
  min_height: 120
)
```

Alice is tall enough (Right) but too young (Left):

```
iex> FunPark.Ride.FastLane.ensure_height(alice, haunted_mansion)
%FunPark.Monad.Either.Right{
  right: %FunPark.Patron{name: "Alice", age: 12, height: 125, ... }
}

iex> FunPark.Ride.FastLane.ensure_age(alice, haunted_mansion)
%FunPark.Monad.Either.Left{
    left: %FunPark.Errors.ValidationError{
      errors: ["Alice is not old enough"]
  }
}
```

Inside the Left, we have the context of the failure and a ValidationError—along with a human-readable message.

When we check Beth, although she meets the age requirement, she is too short:

```
iex> FunPark.Ride.FastLane.ensure_age(beth, haunted_mansion)
%FunPark.Monad.Either.Right{
  right: %FunPark.Patron{ name: "Beth", age: 16, height: 115, ... }
}

iex> FunPark.Ride.FastLane.ensure_height(beth, haunted_mansion)
%FunPark.Monad.Either.Left{
  left: %FunPark.Errors.ValidationError{
    errors: ["Beth is not tall enough"]
  }
}
```

While it's helpful to be able to check a single business rule, what we really need is the ability to combine rules.

## Combining Eligibility

Since Either is a monad, we can chain our Kleisli functions using bind/2:

```
lib/fun_park/ride/fast_lane.ex
def ensure_eligibility(%Patron{} = patron, %Ride{} = ride) do
  validate_height = curry_r(&ensure_height/2)

  patron
  |> ensure_age(ride)
  |> bind(validate_height.(ride))
end
```

When we chain functions with bind/2, we progressively narrow the context—in this case, from a Patron to an EitherEligiblePatron.

At this point, neither Alice nor Beth is eligible, but for different reasons:

```
iex> FunPark.Ride.FastLane.ensure_eligibility(alice, haunted_mansion)
%FunPark.Monad.Either.Left{
  left: %FunPark.Errors.ValidationError{
    errors: ["Alice is not old enough"]
  }
}

iex> FunPark.Ride.FastLane.ensure_eligibility(beth, haunted_mansion)
%FunPark.Monad.Either.Left{
  left: %FunPark.Errors.ValidationError{
    errors: ["Beth is not tall enough"]
  }
}
```

Let's look at Charles, who is both too young and too short:

```
iex> charles = FunPark.Patron.make( "Charles", 13, 115)

iex> FunPark.Ride.FastLane.ensure_eligibility(charles, haunted_mansion)
%FunPark.Monad.Either.Left{
  left: %FunPark.Errors.ValidationError{
    errors: ["Charles is not old enough"]
  }
}
```

With bind/2, as soon as we determine that Charles is too young, any remaining checks are skipped. We don't need to evaluate whether Charles is tall enough if we've ruled him out based on age.

Now let's check Dave:

```
iex> dave = FunPark.Patron.make( "Dave", 16, 140)
```

Dave meets the ride's eligibility criteria:

```
iex> FunPark.Ride.FastLane.ensure_eligibility(dave, haunted_mansion)
%FunPark.Monad.Either.Right{
  right: %FunPark.Patron{ name: "Dave", age: 16, height: 140, ... }
}
```

Next, let's check if he can use the fast lane.

## Ensure a FastPass

Like our ride eligibility logic, we can reuse our fast_pass?/2 predicate.

lib/fun_park/ride/fast_lane.ex
```
def ensure_fast_pass(%Patron{} = patron, %Ride{} = ride) do
  patron
  |> Either.lift_predicate(
    curry_r(&Ride.fast_pass?/2).(ride),
    fn p -> "#{Patron.get_name(p)} does not have a fast pass" end
  )
  |> Either.map_left(&ValidationError.new/1)
end
```

Here, we lift our Ride.fast_pass?/2 predicate, and on Left, map the error to the ValidationError struct.

## Run it

Dave is eligible to ride the Haunted Mansion, but he does not have a FastPass.

```
iex> FunPark.Ride.FastLane.ensure_fast_pass(dave, haunted_mansion)
%FunPark.Monad.Either.Left{
  left: %FunPark.Errors.ValidationError{
    errors: ["Dave does not have a fast pass"]
  }
}
```

Let's give him one:

```
iex> datetime = DateTime.new!(~D[2025-06-01], ~T[13:00:00])
iex> fast_pass = FunPark.FastPass.make(haunted_mansion, datetime)
iex> dave = FunPark.Patron.add_fast_pass(dave, fast_pass)
```

Now, Dave can enter the Haunted Mansion's fast lane:

```
iex> FunPark.Ride.FastLane.ensure_fast_pass(dave, haunted_mansion)
%FunPark.Monad.Either.Right{right: %FunPark.Patron{ name: "Dave", ...}}
```

But what about Elsie? She doesn't have a FastPass, but she is a VIP:

```
iex> elsie = FunPark.Patron.make( "Elsie", 17, 135, ticket_tier: :vip)

iex> FunPark.Ride.FastLane.ensure_fast_pass(elsie, haunted_mansion)
%FunPark.Monad.Either.Left{
  left: %FunPark.Errors.ValidationError{
    errors: ["Elsie does not have a fast pass"]
  }
}
```

This is a mistake; we know from our Ride expert that a VIP doesn't need a pass to use the fast lane.

## Ensure a FastPass or VIP Access

We need to ensure a patron can enter if they have a valid FastPass *or* VIP status.

lib/fun_park/ride/fast_lane.ex
```
def ensure_vip_or_fast_pass(%Patron{} = patron, %Ride{} = ride) do
  patron
  |> Either.lift_predicate(
    &Patron.vip?/1,
    fn p -> "#{Patron.get_name(p)} is not a VIP" end
  )
  |> Either.map_left(&ValidationError.new/1)
  |> Either.or_else(fn -> ensure_fast_pass(patron, ride) end)
end
```

As we did with Maybe, we use the disjunctive or_else/2 to recover.

Now, with her VIP status, Elsie has access to the fast lane:

```
iex> FunPark.Ride.FastLane.ensure_vip_or_fast_pass(elsie, haunted_mansion)
%FunPark.Monad.Either.Right{
  right: %FunPark.Patron{ name: "Elsie", ticket_tier: :vip, ... }
}
```

## Ensure Fast Lane Access

We don't want patrons entering the fast lane only to be turned away at the ride itself. To avoid this, we need to chain the eligibility checks, ensuring that patrons are both eligible for the ride and hold a valid FastPass.

lib/fun_park/ride/fast_lane.ex
```elixir
def ensure_fast_pass_lane(%Patron{} = patron, %Ride{} = ride) do
  ensure_vip_or_pass = curry_r(&ensure_vip_or_fast_pass/2)

  patron
  |> ensure_eligibility(ride)fast
  |> bind(ensure_vip_or_pass.(ride))
end
```

Again, we're dealing with Kleisli functions—we can bind them together to conjunctively narrow our context. Now we have EitherFastPassLane, where patrons are both eligible and are either VIP or have a valid FastPass.

## Run It

Let's see if our patrons can enter the fast lane:

```elixir
iex> FunPark.Ride.FastLane.ensure_fast_pass_lane(alice, haunted_mansion)
%FunPark.Monad.Either.Left{
  left: %FunPark.Errors.ValidationError{
    errors: ["Alice is not old enough"]
  }
}

iex> FunPark.Ride.FastLane.ensure_fast_pass_lane(beth, haunted_mansion)
%FunPark.Monad.Either.Left{
  left: %FunPark.Errors.ValidationError{
    errors: ["Beth is not tall enough"]
  }
}

iex> FunPark.Ride.FastLane.ensure_fast_pass_lane(charles, haunted_mansion)
%FunPark.Monad.Either.Left{
  left: %FunPark.Errors.ValidationError{
    errors: ["Charles is not old enough"]
  }
}

iex> FunPark.Ride.FastLane.ensure_fast_pass_lane(dave, haunted_mansion)
%FunPark.Monad.Either.Right{ right: %FunPark.Patron{ name: "Dave", ... }}

iex> FunPark.Ride.FastLane.ensure_fast_pass_lane(elsie, haunted_mansion)
%FunPark.Monad.Either.Right{ right: %FunPark.Patron{ name: "Elsie", ... }}
```

With ensure_fast_pass_lane/2, we protect our fast lane but also give information about why a patron was rejected.

## Ensure Groups of Patrons

As we learned from our Ride expert, sometimes groups of patrons want to ride together. In this case, we need to ensure that every member of the group qualifies before allowing them into the fast lane.

As we did in Maybe, we can do this with traverse/2, which takes a list and a Kleisli function and performs a monadic traversal. If all results are Right, the result is Right(list_of_patrons). If any result is a Left, the traversal short-circuits and returns Left(reason).

```
lib/fun_park/ride/fast_lane.ex
def ensure_fast_pass_lane_group(
      patrons,
      %Ride{} = ride
    )
    when is_list(patrons) do
  eligible_for_fast_lane = curry_r(&ensure_fast_pass_lane/2)

  Either.traverse(
    patrons,
    eligible_for_fast_lane.(ride)
  )
end
```

Here, we traverse the list of patrons using our eligible_for_fast_lane/2 Kleisli function—checking one patron at a time and short-circuiting if any check fails.

## Run It

As a group, Elsie and Dave can enter the Haunted Mansion's fast lane:

```
iex> patrons = [elsie, dave]
iex> FunPark.Ride.FastLane.ensure_fast_pass_lane_group(
  patrons,
  haunted_mansion
)
%FunPark.Monad.Either.Right{
  right: [
    %FunPark.Patron{ name: "Elsie", ... }
    %FunPark.Patron{ name: "Dave", ... }
  ]
}
```

But Charles cannot:

```
iex> patrons = [elsie, dave, charles]
iex> FunPark.Ride.FastLane.ensure_fast_pass_lane_group(
  patrons,
  haunted_mansion
)
```

```
%FunPark.Monad.Either.Left{
  left: %FunPark.Errors.ValidationError{
    errors: ["Charles is not old enough"]
  }
}
```

If we add patrons after Charles, it still fails the same way:

```
iex> patrons = [elsie, dave, charles, beth]
iex> FunPark.Ride.FastLane.ensure_fast_pass_lane_group(
  patrons,
  haunted_mansion
)
%FunPark.Monad.Either.Left{
  left: %FunPark.Errors.ValidationError{
    errors: ["Charles is not old enough"]
  }
}
```

This is because after determining Charles is not eligible, we don't need to check Beth.

Notice that if we swap Charles and Beth, then Beth's ineligibility is the one we'll see:

```
iex> patrons = [elsie, dave, beth, charles]
iex> FunPark.Ride.FastLane.ensure_fast_pass_lane_group(
  patrons,
  haunted_mansion
)
%FunPark.Monad.Either.Left{
  left: %FunPark.Errors.ValidationError{
    errors: ["Beth is not tall enough"]
  }
}
```

Monads are useful for dependent steps and for expensive operations where early failure avoids unnecessary work. But sometimes we want to run multiple checks independently and collect all the results, not just the first failure.

## From Bind to Combine

Our Ride expert is back with a new concern. Right now, patrons only see the first reason they were denied access to the fast lane. As a result, they might not know everything they need to address before becoming eligible. The problem is even worse for groups: a family might have Alice stay back with her mom, only to find out later that Beth was also ineligible—leaving everyone frustrated.

To solve this, we need to move from a monadic traversal, which stops at the first Left, to an applicative traversal, which runs the checks independently and collects the results into an Either—Right(list_of_results) if all succeed or Left(list_of_reasons) if any fail.

lib/fun_park/monad/either.ex
```
def traverse_a([], _func), do: right([])

def traverse_a(list, func) when is_list(list) and is_function(func, 1) do
  fold_l(list, right([]), fn item, acc_result ->
    case {func.(item), acc_result} do
      {%Right{right: value}, %Right{right: acc}} ->
        right([value | acc])

      {%Left{left: new}, %Left{left: existing}} ->
        left(append(existing, coerce(new)))

      {%Right{}, %Left{left: existing}} ->
        left(existing)

      {%Left{left: err}, %Right{}} ->
        left(coerce(err))
    end
  end)
  |> map(&:lists.reverse/1)
end
```

Here, traverse_a/2 applies a function to each item in the list, collecting either successes or errors. Because Either is right-biased, traversal begins in a Right state and can flip to Left—but never back. If every item succeeds, their results are collected into a Right. If any item fails, the state flips to Left, discards prior successes, and begins accumulating errors. From that point on, only errors are collected.

We are collecting results in traverse_a/2, so it's helpful to implement an *appendable* structure, one that knows how to collect results.

lib/fun_park/appendable.ex
```
defprotocol FunPark.Appendable do
  @fallback_to_any true

  def coerce(term)

  def append(accumulator, coerced)
end
```

The Appendable protocol defines a generic interface for combining values of the same kind.

- coerce/1 transforms a raw value into a form that can participate in combination.
- append/2 defines how two coerced values should be combined.

A fallback implementation is provided for unrecognized types, using @fallback_to_any true. This default treats values as list-like: if a term isn't explicitly handled by a struct-based implementation, it gets coerced into a list and appended using standard list concatenation.

lib/fun_park/appendable.ex
```
defimpl FunPark.Appendable, for: Any do
  def coerce(value) when is_list(value), do: value
  def coerce(value), do: [value]

  def append(acc, value), do: coerce(acc) ++ coerce(value)
end
```

Now we can implement the Appendable protocol for the ValidationError struct:

lib/fun_park/errors/validation_error.ex
```
defimpl FunPark.Appendable, for: FunPark.Errors.ValidationError do
  alias FunPark.Errors.ValidationError

  def coerce(%ValidationError{errors: e}), do: ValidationError.new(e)

  def append(%ValidationError{} = acc, %ValidationError{} = value) do
    ValidationError.merge(acc, value)
  end
end
```

- coerce/1 calls new/1, ensuring the errors field is always a list.
- append/2 combines two ValidationError structs, using merge/2.

By pushing aggregation behavior behind the Appendable protocol, the traversal logic remains decoupled from how values are combined. New accumulation strategies can be introduced by implementing Appendable for a different struct, without changing the traversal itself. This follows the *open/closed principle*: traverse_a/2 is closed for modification but open to extension.

> If this looks a bit like a Monoid, you're right—it follows a similar mental model: combining things in an associative way.

## Run It

Let's return to our patrons and ride:

```
iex> alice = FunPark.Patron.make( "Alice", 12, 125, ticket_tier: :vip)
iex> beth = FunPark.Patron.make( "Beth", 16, 115)
iex> charles = FunPark.Patron.make( "Charles", 13, 115)
iex> dave = FunPark.Patron.make( "Dave", 16, 140)
iex> elsie = FunPark.Patron.make( "Elsie", 17, 135, ticket_tier: :vip)

iex> haunted_mansion = FunPark.Ride.make(
  "Haunted Mansion",
  min_age: 14,
  min_height: 120
)
```

Next, let's reuse our ride eligibility logic.

```
iex> valid_height = FunPark.Utils.curry_r(
  &FunPark.Ride.FastLane.ensure_height/2
)
iex> valid_age = FunPark.Utils.curry_r(&FunPark.Ride.FastLane.ensure_age/2)
```

But instead of chaining them one at a time, create a list of validators.

```
iex> validators = [
  valid_height.(haunted_mansion),
  valid_age.(haunted_mansion)
]
```

Earlier we learned that we traverse a list of patrons (state) with a Kleisli function. But we can also traverse a list of Kleisli functions with a function that applies state.

> We're flipping the mental model here. We're no longer checking many things—we're checking one thing many ways. It's the same structure, just turned inside out.

```
iex> FunPark.Monad.Either.traverse_a(validators, & &1.(alice))
%FunPark.Monad.Either.Left{
  left: %FunPark.Errors.ValidationError{
    errors: ["Alice is not old enough"]
  }
}
```

Here we traversed over our validators and applied them to Alice, to find she's not old enough.

Let's apply them to Beth, who is too short:

```
iex> FunPark.Monad.Either.traverse_a(validators, & &1.(beth))
%FunPark.Monad.Either.Left{
  left: %FunPark.Errors.ValidationError{
    errors: ["Beth is not tall enough"]
  }
}
```

Charles is both too short and too young:

```
iex> FunPark.Monad.Either.traverse_a(validators, & &1.(charles))
%FunPark.Monad.Either.Left{
  left: %FunPark.Errors.ValidationError{
    errors: ["Charles is not tall enough", "Charles is not old enough"]
  }
}
```

Let's check Dave, who is eligible:

```
iex> FunPark.Monad.Either.traverse_a(validators, & &1.(dave))
%FunPark.Monad.Either.Right{
  right: [
    %FunPark.Patron{ name: "Dave", ... },
    %FunPark.Patron{ name: "Dave", ... },
  ]
}
```

Both validity checks passed, but we ended up with a list of Daves, which isn't right. traverse_a/2 returns all successes or all errors, but what we want here is validation: applying a series of independent checks to a single value and returning either that value or a list of errors.

lib/fun_park/monad/either.ex
```
def validate(value, validators) when is_list(validators) do
  traverse_a(validators, fn validator -> validator.(value) end)
  |> map(fn _ -> value end)
end
```

validate/2 applies a list of validations using traverse_a/2, then uses map/2 to transform the list of successes back into the original value.

Here, Dave is eligible:

```
iex> FunPark.Monad.Either.validate(dave, validators)
%FunPark.Monad.Either.Right{
  right: %FunPark.Patron{ name: "Dave", ... }
}
```

And again, Charles is not:

```
iex> FunPark.Monad.Either.validate(charles, validators)
%FunPark.Monad.Either.Left{
  left: %FunPark.Errors.ValidationError{
    errors: ["Charles is not tall enough", "Charles is not old enough"]
  }
}
```

Notice we still have a Kleisli function: validate/2 takes a value and returns a monad. We can continue composing with it to solve even more complex problems. But first, let's save our logic to the Ride module:

lib/fun_park/ride/fast_lane.ex
```
def validate_eligibility(%Patron{} = patron, %Ride{} = ride) do
  validate_height = curry_r(&ensure_height/2)
  validate_age = curry_r(&ensure_age/2)
  patron
  |> Either.validate([validate_height.(ride), validate_age.(ride)])
end
```

As usual, our Ride expert has a new note—the fast lane should only allow patrons if the ride is online.

lib/fun_park/ride.ex
```
def ensure_online(%__MODULE__{} = ride) do
  Either.lift_predicate(
    ride,
    &online?/1,
    fn r -> "#{r.name} is offline" end
  )
  |> Either.map_left(&ValidationError.new/1)
end
```

We can compose eligibility, the FastPass check, and a ride's online status to establish our fast-line validation.

```
def validate_fast_pass_lane(%Patron{} = patron, %Ride{} = ride) do
  validate_eligibility = curry(&validate_eligibility/2)
  validate_vip_or_pass = curry(&ensure_vip_or_fast_pass/2)
  Either.validate(
    ride,
    [
      validate_eligibility.(patron),
      validate_vip_or_pass.(patron),
      &Ride.ensure_online/1
    ]
  )
  |> map(fn _ -> patron end)
end
```

Notice that ensure_online/1 only checks the ride, so we need to shift validation from the patron to the ride. As a result, the function returns the ride rather than the patron. That's an easy fix: use map/2 to transform the Right result to the Patron while leaving the Left unchanged.

## Run It

Alice is a VIP, so she doesn't need a FastPass—but she's still too young:

```
iex> FunPark.Ride.FastLane.validate_fast_pass_lane(alice, haunted_mansion)
%FunPark.Monad.Either.Left{
  left: %FunPark.Errors.ValidationError{
    errors: ["Alice is not old enough"]
  }
}
```

Beth is too short and lacks a FastPass:

```
iex> FunPark.Ride.FastLane.validate_fast_pass_lane(beth, haunted_mansion)
%FunPark.Monad.Either.Left{
  left: %FunPark.Errors.ValidationError{
    errors: ["Beth is not tall enough", "Beth does not have a fast pass"]
  }
}
```

Charles is neither tall enough nor old enough, and he also doesn't have a FastPass:

```
iex> FunPark.Ride.FastLane.validate_fast_pass_lane(charles, haunted_mansion)
%FunPark.Monad.Either.Left{
  left: %FunPark.Errors.ValidationError{
    errors: [
      "Charles is not tall enough",
      "Charles is not old enough",
      "Charles does not have a fast pass"
    ]
  }
}
```

Dave is tall enough and old enough—but doesn't have a FastPass:

```
iex> FunPark.Ride.FastLane.validate_fast_pass_lane(dave, haunted_mansion)
%FunPark.Monad.Either.Left{
  left: %FunPark.Errors.ValidationError{
    errors: ["Dave does not have a fast pass"]
  }
}
```

Let's give him one:

```
iex> datetime = DateTime.new!(~D[2025-06-01], ~T[13:00:00])
iex> fast_pass = FunPark.FastPass.make(haunted_mansion, datetime)
iex> dave = FunPark.Patron.add_fast_pass(dave, fast_pass)
```

Now Dave can enter the Haunted Mansion's fast lane:

```
iex> FunPark.Ride.FastLane.validate_fast_pass_lane(dave, haunted_mansion)
%FunPark.Monad.Either.Right{
  right: %FunPark.Patron{ name: "Dave", ... }
}
```

And finally, Elsie—who is eligible and a VIP—can enter the fast lane:

```
iex> FunPark.Ride.FastLane.validate_fast_pass_lane(elsie, haunted_mansion)
%FunPark.Monad.Either.Right{
  right: %FunPark.Patron{ name: "Elsie", ... }
}
```

But if we take Haunted Mansion offline:

```
iex> haunted_mansion = FunPark.Ride.change(
  haunted_mansion,
  %{online: false}
)
%FunPark.Ride{ name: "Haunted Mansion", online: false, ... }
```

She can no longer enter the fast lane:

```
iex> FunPark.Ride.FastLane.validate_fast_pass_lane(elsie, haunted_mansion)
%FunPark.Monad.Either.Left{
  left: %FunPark.Errors.ValidationError{
    errors: ["Haunted Mansion is offline"]
  }
}
```

## Don't Look, Just Fly

Time to resolve our Ride expert's concern: a group of patrons can enter the fast lane together but only if all of them qualify. We need to either admit the entire group or return every reason they cannot enter. (The code is on the next page.)

lib/fun_park/ride/fast_lane.ex
```
def validate_fast_pass_lane_group(
      patrons,
      %Ride{} = ride
    )
    when is_list(patrons) do
  validate_fast_lane = curry_r(&validate_fast_pass_lane/2)

  patrons
  |> Either.traverse_a(validate_fast_lane.(ride))
end
```

Behind the scenes, we're calling a traverse_a/2 inside another traverse_a/2, trusting that composition will work—that each layer will stack cleanly without extra coordination. That trust extends further down the stack: we rely on appendables to combine validation results and on monoids to combine predicates that express the domain rules. This is the essence of functional programming: small, predictable parts that compose, letting us layer logic upon logic.

## Run It

Let's see if our patrons can ride the Haunted Mansion together:

```
iex> haunted_mansion = FunPark.Ride.change(
  haunted_mansion,
  %{online: true}
)
iex> patrons = [alice, beth, charles, dave, elsie]
iex> FunPark.Ride.FastLane.validate_fast_pass_lane_group(
  patrons,
  haunted_mansion
)
%FunPark.Monad.Either.Left{
  left: %FunPark.Errors.ValidationError{
    errors: [
      "Alice is not old enough",
      "Beth is not tall enough",
      "Beth does not have a fast pass",
      "Charles is not tall enough",
      "Charles is not old enough",
      "Charles does not have a fast pass"
    ]
  }
}
```

They can't, but it looks like Dave and Elsie can:

```
iex> patrons = [dave, elsie]
iex> FunPark.Ride.FastLane.validate_fast_pass_lane_group(
  patrons,
  haunted_mansion
)
%FunPark.Monad.Either.Right{
  right: [
    %FunPark.Patron{ name: "Dave", ... },
    %FunPark.Patron{ name: "Elsie", ... }
  ]
}
```

### Act on It

Eric Evans coined the term *supple model* to describe a design that starts with raw materials that are hammered into form as our domain understanding deepens. In functional programming, those raw materials are small, composable functions—each solving a narrow piece of the domain. Through composition, we hammer those fragments into structure, shaping them as our understanding evolves.

How might you hammer out the following situations?

- You only need to know whether the patron is eligible for the ride, not why. How might you reduce multiple messages to a single "Alice is not eligible"?
- How might you validate a patron, but only if the ride is online?
- A patron might not qualify for the fast lane but still be allowed to ride. How might you return either "Alice is not eligible for this ride" or "Alice can ride, but not through the fast lane"?

Find the Either Chapter Answers, on page 216.

## Make Errors Explicit

Joe Armstrong, one of the creators of Erlang, and Philip Wadler, a key contributor to Haskell, had fundamentally different views on error handling. Armstrong embraced a "let it crash" philosophy: if something goes wrong, let the process fail and rely on a supervisor to recover. Wadler, by contrast, argued that success and failure should live within a single control flow.

But in practice, there's no one-size-fits-all. Sometimes we want to recover—handle the failure gracefully and continue. Other times, failure means something has gone irreparably wrong, and crashing is the right choice. What matters is choosing the right strategy for the situation—and making that choice explicit in the code.

Take ETS: an in-memory key-value store built into the Erlang runtime. As Joe Armstrong describes in *Programming Erlang [Arm13]*, ETS is designed for performance and simplicity—and it follows the Erlang fault philosophy. If something goes wrong, it raises an error and crashes the process. By wrapping ETS calls in Either, we bring that failure into our structure. Instead of crashing, we represent it as "this call carries the *possibility* of success."

Some failures are the caller's responsibility to prevent, like ensuring each item has an :id. We treat these as broken invariants and let them crash. Other failures—like a missing table—we handle within Either, assuming the caller has the ability to recover.

## A Store for FunPark

Let's implement FunPark's store using ETS, explicitly handling uncertainty with the Either monad.

### Create Table

We begin by defining a function to create a new ETS table:

lib/fun_park/store.ex
```
def create_table(table) when is_atom(table) do
  Either.from_try(fn ->
    :ets.new(table, [:named_table, :set, :public])
  end)
end
```

ETS doesn't guarantee that a table will be created; it raises an error if the table already exists. Here, we wrap that behavior, returning Right(table_id) on success and Left(error) on failure. Also, notice when_atom/1, a refinement in the function head. This serves as an invariant, crashing immediately if violated.

### Delete Table

Next, we define a way to drop the table:

lib/fun_park/store.ex
```
def drop_table(table) when is_atom(table) do
  Either.from_try(fn ->
    :ets.delete(table)
  end)
  |> map(fn _ -> table end)
end
```

Again, ETS raises an error if the table doesn't exist. This function catches that case and returns a Left(error) instead.

**Insert Item**

To add items to the store, we define an insert function:

```
lib/fun_park/store.ex
def insert_item(table, %{id: id} = item) when is_atom(table) do
  Either.from_try(fn ->
    :ets.insert(table, {id, Map.from_struct(item)})
  end)
  |> map(fn _ -> item end)
end
```

Here, we assume each item has an :id. That's the caller's responsibility. If it's missing, the function crashes—it's a broken invariant, not something we try to recover from. Other failures, like inserting into a nonexistent table, are returned as Left(error).

Before storage, we strip metadata from the struct—it doesn't belong in the raw data layer.

ETS's insert/2 returns true on success or raises an error on failure. But Right(true) isn't meaningful—Right already signals success, so true adds no useful information. To preserve composability, we map over the result and replace true with the original item, returning a structure suitable for monadic composition.

**Get Item**

Here, we retrieve an item by ID:

```
lib/fun_park/store.ex
def get_item(table, id) when is_atom(table) do
  Either.from_try(fn ->
    :ets.lookup(table, id)
  end)
  |> bind(fn
    [{_id, item}] -> Either.pure(item)
    [] -> Either.left(:not_found)
  end)
end
```

Depending on whether the item exists, ETS returns either a one-element list or an empty list. We treat those results as a success (Right(item)) or absence (Left(:not_found)). And if the table is missing, we pass the Left(error) along.

### Get All Items

And here, we retrieve all items from the table:

lib/fun_park/store.ex
```
def get_all_items(table) when is_atom(table) do
  Either.from_try(fn ->
    :ets.tab2list(table)
  end)
  |> map(fn items ->
    Enum.map(items, fn {_, item} -> item end)
  end)
end
```

On failure, it returns a Left(error). On success, it transforms each {id, item} tuple to item.

### Delete Item

Finally, we remove an item by ID:

lib/fun_park/store.ex
```
def delete_item(table, id) when is_atom(table) do
  Either.from_try(fn ->
    :ets.delete(table, id)
  end)
  |> map(fn _ -> id end)
end
```

Like the other functions, delete_item/2 wraps ETS behavior in Either. A missing table becomes Left(error), and a successful deletion returns Right(id).

## Ride Repository

In domain-driven design, a repository serves as a gateway between the domain and the data store. It hides persistence details and protects the model's integrity by enforcing validation before data is written.

If you've used the *Ecto library [WM19]*, you've seen a repo in action.

Here we're going to define a repository for our Ride context.

### Create a Table

First, we need to create the table to store our rides:

lib/fun_park/ride/repo.ex
```
def create_table do
  Store.create_table(@table_name)
end
```

### Save a Ride

Before saving, we validate our Ride:

lib/fun_park/ride.ex
```
def validate(%__MODULE__{} = ride) do
  Either.validate(
    ride,
    [
      &ensure_min_age/1,
      &ensure_min_height/1,
      &ensure_wait_time/1,
      &ensure_name/1
    ]
  )
end
```

Now, only validated rides will be written to the store:

lib/fun_park/ride/repo.ex
```
def save(%Ride{} = ride) do
  insert_ride = curry(&Store.insert_item/2)

  ride
  |> Ride.validate()
  |> bind(insert_ride.(@table_name))
end
```

### Get a Ride

To fetch a ride by ID, we retrieve the record and reconstruct a valid struct:

lib/fun_park/ride/repo.ex
```
def get(id) when is_integer(id) do
  Store.get_item(@table_name, id)
  |> map(fn data -> struct(Ride, data) end)
  |> Either.map_left(fn _ -> :not_found end)
end
```

Notice the use of map_left/2, which replaces any failure reason with :not_found. Here, we're deliberately collapsing all failure cases into one—assuming the Ride context only cares that the data *is* missing, not *why* it's missing.

### Get All Rides

To list rides, we load all entries, reconstruct each struct, and sort them by name:

lib/fun_park/ride/repo.ex
```
def list() do
  Store.get_all_items(@table_name)
  |> map(fn items ->
    items
```

```
  |> Enum.map(fn item -> struct(Ride, item) end)
  |> List.sort()
end)
|> Either.get_or_else([])
end
```

Here we can use get_or_else/2, which collapses the possibility of a list into a guaranteed list. Again, we're assuming the Ride context only cares that there *is* no data—not *why* there's no data.

### Delete a Ride

Deletion is treated as best-effort:

```
lib/fun_park/ride/repo.ex
def delete(%Ride{id: id}) do
  Store.delete_item(@table_name, id)
  |> Either.get_or_else(:ok)
end
```

Whether the ride is missing or the deletion fails, the result is always :ok. We're assuming the Ride context doesn't care whether the deletion succeeded or why it may have failed.

## Run It

Let's start by creating our table:

```
iex> FunPark.Ride.Repo.create_table()
%FunPark.Monad.Either.Right{right: :rides}
```

Next, we generate a couple of rides:

```
iex> banana = FunPark.Ride.make("Banana Slip")
iex> apple = FunPark.Ride.make("Apple Cart")
```

With the repository, we can save valid rides to our store:

```
iex> FunPark.Ride.Repo.save(banana)
%FunPark.Monad.Either.Right{
  right: %FunPark.Ride{id: 8, name: "Banana Slip", ... }
}

iex> FunPark.Ride.Repo.save(apple)
%FunPark.Monad.Either.Right{
  right: %FunPark.Ride{id: 40, name: "Apple Cart", ... }
}
```

Say we create an invalid ride:

```
iex> bad_apple = FunPark.Ride.change(apple, %{wait_time: -1, min_age: -1})
%FunPark.Ride{
  id: 40,
  name: "Apple Cart",
  min_age: -1,
  wait_time: -1,
  ...
}
```

We get Left, informing us that it did not save, because of a validation error:

```
iex> FunPark.Ride.Repo.save(bad_apple)
%FunPark.Monad.Either.Left{
  left: %FunPark.Errors.ValidationError{
    errors: ["Apple Cart: min age must be non negative",
     "Apple Cart: wait time must be non negative"]
  }
}
```

We can retrieve our saved rides:

```
iex> FunPark.Ride.Repo.get(banana.id)
%FunPark.Monad.Either.Right{
  right: %FunPark.Ride{ id: 8, name: "Banana Slip", ... }
}
iex> FunPark.Ride.Repo.get(apple.id)
%FunPark.Monad.Either.Right{
  right: %FunPark.Ride{ id: 40, name: "Apple Cart", ... }
}
```

Or we get a list of all rides in their domain order:

```
iex> FunPark.Ride.Repo.list()
[
  %FunPark.Ride{ id: 40, name: "Apple Cart", ... },
  %FunPark.Ride{ id: 8, name: "Banana Slip", ... }
]
```

The results of list/0 are not wrapped in Either, because our repository is recovering from a potential storage error with an empty list.

Say we delete the Apple Cart ride:

```
iex> FunPark.Ride.Repo.delete(apple)
:ok
```

It becomes :not_found:

```
iex> FunPark.Ride.Repo.get(apple.id)
%FunPark.Monad.Either.Left{left: :not_found}
```

Because our delete operation is idempotent, we can delete it multiple times:

```
iex> FunPark.Ride.Repo.delete(apple)
:ok

iex> FunPark.Ride.Repo.delete(apple)
:ok
```

Let's say another process deletes the entire table:

```
iex> FunPark.Store.drop_table(:rides)
%FunPark.Monad.Either.Right{right: :ok}
```

The Ride context can still delete:

```
iex> FunPark.Ride.Repo.delete(apple)
:ok
```

And the caller doesn't care that the table has been dropped, only that the ride isn't available:

```
iex> FunPark.Ride.Repo.get(apple.id)
%FunPark.Monad.Either.Left{left: :not_found}
```

Also, it doesn't care *why* there are no rides, just that the outcome is an empty list:

```
iex> FunPark.Ride.Repo.list()
[]
```

By lifting ETS into Either, we reframe failure handling to match the needs of our context.

Note that many Erlang and Elixir libraries already use in-band error handling via tagged tuples like {:ok, result} and {:error, reason}. Either follows the same spirit but replaces tuples with structs and adds composability through monadic operations.

Our goal is to raise errors for broken invariants, failures with no path forward. But when uncertainty is expected, we model it explicitly, giving the caller a chance to see the problem and choose how to recover.

# What You've Learned

This chapter was more challenging—not because Either is more complex than Maybe (it's not) but because it raised the level of abstraction.

We tackled validation, not by introducing a new concept but by building on what we already knew. We began by lifting predicates—this time into a context that carried a reason alongside the decision. We extended this to groups, using traversal to short-circuit and return the first failure. That uncovered a new challenge: how to accumulate independent failures, leading us to a new mental model—the applicative sequence.

Earlier, we treated interops as a way to *cut in*, applying functional concepts in isolation. In this chapter, we went further: using them to reframe an existing library, lift entire subsystems, and gain composable, monadic control flow.

Most importantly, we began moving from *seeing* patterns to *trusting* them—trusting them to hold their shape, support composition, and recede into the background as our attention shifts to higher-level concerns. Scott Wlaschin calls this Railway Oriented Programming: connecting track segments into routes, and routes into networks.[2]

Either gives us a way to model uncertainty inside the program, capturing success and failure within the control flow. But some operations reach beyond the program itself: querying an external database, writing to a file, making an HTTP request. These are side effects—and by their nature, they take time. To manage side effects, we need a new abstraction: the Effect.

> This chapter is about transfer and refinement—that's how we build expertise. If things aren't clicking yet, go back and keep digging into the previous concepts. We don't get better just by repeating something. We get better by spotting what's not working, improving it, and trying again.

---

2.  https://fsharpforfunandprofit.com/rop

# CHAPTER 10

# Coordinate Tasks with Effect

> A production-ready Effect is available in the Funx library.[1]

You click Print—and nothing happens.

Did the printer jam? Is it even on? Maybe the network dropped. Interactions with the outside world are unpredictable. These are *side effects*: actions that reach beyond the program, often referred to as input–output (I/O).

Side effects depend on external conditions, so the same call can yield different results. This breaks referential transparency, anathema to functional programming.

Philip Wadler proposed a solution in 1995: instead of executing effects directly, model them as instructions and defer execution to a controlled boundary.[2] While side effects are inherently impure, the instructions for producing them can remain pure.

Elixir developers typically manage I/O using Task, a lightweight abstraction built on Erlang's process model.

From a purely functional perspective, Task is problematic: it runs eagerly, breaks the separation between definition and execution, and raises errors instead of keeping them in context. Also, orchestrating tasks—especially with nested or branching logic—can be error prone.

---

1.  https://hexdocs.pm/funx/Funx.Monad.Effect.html
2.  https://homepages.inf.ed.ac.uk/wadler/papers/marktoberdorf/baastad.pdf

Inspired by Scala's ZIO, our Effect extends Wadler's formulation by using Either to represent success or failure and Reader to provide a shared environment.[3]

In this chapter, we'll explore how to implement the Effect monad in Elixir and revisit our Store, transforming it from the Either context to the Effect context.

## Build the Effect

The ZIO library implements Effect as a sequential abstraction. Concurrency requires special handling through fibers or explicit parallel combinators. As a result, branching logic always happens *after* the Effect has been evaluated.

We have the opposite problem. Our Effect is concurrent by default. Instead of making sequential code run concurrently, we need ways to make concurrent code run sequentially.

Elixir favors pattern matching, and some problems, particularly traversing, are easier to express with top-level Effect.Right and Effect.Left. So unlike ZIO, our Effect includes branching as part of its structure.

```
lib/fun_park/monad/effect/right.ex
def pure(value) do
  %__MODULE__{
    effect: fn _env ->
      Task.async(fn -> Either.pure(value) end)
    end
  }
end
```

Here, Right.pure/1 creates an Effect struct with a deferred function that returns an asynchronous task. When executed, the task produces an Either.Right, wrapping the given value and representing success.

To represent failure, we have Effect.Left:

```
lib/fun_park/monad/effect/left.ex
def pure(value) do
  %__MODULE__{
    effect: fn _env ->
      Task.async(fn -> Either.left(value) end)
    end
  }
end
```

This works similarly but returns an Either.Left.

---

3.   https://zio.dev/

Like the Reader monad, Right and Left's pure/1 functions pass the environment context down the computation chain.

> In production, effectful code should be observable through telemetry, bounded by timeouts, and isolated to avoid unintended process linkages.

Now that we've defined our structs, we need the protected boundary where we can run an Effect.

lib/fun_park/monad/effect.ex
```elixir
def run(%_{effect: thunk}, env \\ %{}), do: execute_effect(thunk.(env))

defp execute_effect(task) do
  start_time = System.monotonic_time(:millisecond)

  result =
    try do
      case Task.yield(task, 5000) || Task.shutdown(task) do
        {:ok, %Either.Right{} = right} ->
          right

        {:ok, %Either.Left{} = left} ->
          left

        {:ok, other} ->
          Either.left(
            EffectError.new(
              :run,
              {:invalid_result, other}
            )
          )

        nil ->
          Either.left(EffectError.new(:run, :timeout))
      end
    rescue
      error -> Either.left(EffectError.new(:run, error))
    end

  elapsed = System.monotonic_time(:millisecond) - start_time
  IO.puts("Task completed in #{elapsed}ms")

  result
end
```

This extracts the deferred computation, applies the environment, and runs the task with execute_effect/1, which includes a default five-second timeout and logs how long the task takes to complete.

When we run an Effect, several outcomes are possible:

- {:ok, %Either.Right{}}: The task completed and returned a success.
- {:ok, %Either.Left{}}: The task completed and returned a failure.
- {:ok, other}: The task completed, but the result wasn't an Either.
- nil: The task didn't respond within the timeout.
- *Exception:* The task process unexpectedly crashed during execution.

The first two represent expected I/O results. The rest are unexpected, so we wrap them in an EffectError, signaling invalid outputs, timeouts, or crashes.

run/2 is the protected execution boundary for our Effect, preventing unbounded concurrency, isolating crashes, enforcing timeouts, rejecting invalid outputs, and ensuring all failures are captured.

## Run It

Let's start with a basic Effect, wrapping the number 40:

```
iex> effect = FunPark.Monad.Effect.pure(40)
%FunPark.Monad.Effect.Right{
  effect: #Function<...>
}
```

This Effect isn't the number 40—it's a description of a computation to generate the number 40.

Let's run it:

```
iex> FunPark.Monad.Effect.run(effect)
Task completed in 0ms
%FunPark.Monad.Either.Right{right: 40}
```

It succeeded, returning Right(40) in zero milliseconds.

An Elixir Task can fail. For example, we can create an Effect that contains a bomb to crash the underlying process:

```
iex> bomb = fn -> raise "boom" end
iex> bomb_effect = FunPark.Monad.Effect.lift_func(bomb)
%FunPark.Monad.Effect.Right{
  effect: #Function<...>
}
```

Let's run it:

```
iex> FunPark.Monad.Effect.run(bomb_effect)
Task completed in 7ms
```

```
%FunPark.Monad.Either.Left{
  left: %FunPark.Errors.EffectError{
    stage: :lift_func,
    reason: %RuntimeError{message: "boom"}
  }
}
```

We receive a Left, indicating failure. More specifically, it contains an EffectError that signals the failure originated inside the effect's own logic, not from an I/O error. Our lift_func/1 expects the function to be safe, but this one crashed.

An Effect can also fail by timing out. Here's an Effect that takes six seconds, one more than our Task default:

```
iex> long_delay = fn -> Process.sleep(6000) end
iex> long_delay_effect = FunPark.Monad.Effect.lift_func(long_delay)
```

Suppose we run this long task:

```
iex> FunPark.Monad.Effect.run(long_delay_effect)
Task completed in 5003ms
%FunPark.Monad.Either.Left{
  left: %FunPark.Errors.EffectError{stage: :run, reason: :timeout}
}
```

Again, we get a Left with an EffectError, but this time indicating that the failure was from the run stage timing out.

## Implement Protocols

The Effect supports monadic composition with map/2, bind/2, and ap/2. But like Reader, it's a deferred computation, so it doesn't include protocols like Eq, Ord, or Foldable. However, when run, it returns an Either—and Either *can* be compared, ordered, and folded.

## Effect Module

The Effect module provides functions for constructing, inspecting, and lifting into an Effect. These functions mirror those in Maybe and Either but are adapted for deferred computations.

We construct values using right/1, left/1, or pure/1.

Like Reader, access to the environment is through asks/1.

The module includes lifting functions: lift_func/1, lift_either/1, lift_maybe/2, and lift_predicate/3.

It also includes interops: from_result/1, to_result/1, from_try/1, and to_try!/1.

Finally, Effect supports sequencing: traverse/2, sequence/1, traverse_a/2, sequence_a/1, and validate/2.

## Deferred Transformation

With Maybe or Either, the functor transforms a value. With Effect, it describes a deferred transformation.

First, we need our Left:

lib/fun_park/monad/effect/left.ex
```
def map(%Left{} = left, _transform), do: left
```

This indicates the Effect is in a failed state, where it skips the transformation and sends the error forward.

And we need a Right:

lib/fun_park/monad/effect/right.ex
```
def map(%Right{effect: effect}, transform) do
  %Right{
    effect: fn env ->
      Task.async(fn ->
        case Effect.run(%Right{effect: effect}, env) do
          %Either.Right{right: value} ->
            try do
              Either.pure(transform.(value))
            rescue
              e -> Either.left(EffectError.new(:map, e))
            end

          %Either.Left{} = left ->
            left
        end
      end)
    end
  }
end
```

The outer Effect.Right doesn't represent I/O success—that's the role of the inner Either.Right. If the result is Either.Right, the transformation is applied; if it's Either.Left, the transformation is skipped and the failure is propagated.

Transformations should be safe, but more importantly, an Effect must never leak errors. To guarantee this, we rescue unexpected exceptions and wrap them in an EffectError. We could return an Effect.Left here, but since map/2 must preserve structure, we propagate the error within an Effect.Right.

While map/2 doesn't access the Reader environment, it threads it through unchanged, preserving context for subsequent computations.

## Run It

Let's start with the Effect that, when run, returns the value 5 :

```
iex> five_effect = FunPark.Monad.Effect.pure(5)
```

We'll also use a simple function that adds one to the value submitted:

```
iex> increment = fn v -> v + 1 end
```

We can compose a new Effect by mapping increment/1 to five_effect/0 :

```
iex> six_effect = five_effect |> FunPark.Monad.map(increment)
%FunPark.Monad.Effect.Right{
  effect: #Function<...>
}
```

six_effect/0 holds the instructions to first generate the number 5 and then add one.

Now, let's run it in a protected boundary:

```
iex> FunPark.Monad.Effect.run(six_effect)
Task completed in 3ms
Task completed in 4ms
%FunPark.Monad.Either.Right{right: 6}
```

We get Right(6), with the telemetry showing two completed tasks, one from the original pure/1, and one from the transformation applied via map/2.

Let's see what happens when we start with the letter "A":

```
iex> alpha_effect = FunPark.Monad.Effect.pure("A")
```

Now compose it with increment/1:

```
iex> error_effect = alpha_effect |> FunPark.Monad.map(increment)
%FunPark.Monad.Effect.Right{
  effect: #Function<...>
}
```

Take a moment here: effects are pure, even when those instructions include impure operations. This is Philip Wadler's solution for I/O: separate the description of a computation from its execution.

Here, we execute it in our controlled boundary:

```
iex> FunPark.Monad.Effect.run(error_effect)
Task completed in 0ms
Task completed in 2ms
%FunPark.Monad.Either.Left{
  left: %FunPark.Errors.EffectError{
    stage: :map,
    reason: %ArithmeticError{message: "bad argument..."}
  }
}
```

And we get back an Either.Left, indicating that our Effect failed. The map stage had an unexpected ArithmeticError. It turns out that Elixir's + is not pure, which means increment/1 is technically I/O. Let's lift it:

```
iex> increment_effect = FunPark.Monad.Effect.from_try(increment)
```

Here, from_try/1 produces a Kleisli function, changing our increment/1 to a function of type Number -> Effect(Number).

And how do we compose with a Kleisli function? Same as we did in Maybe and Either, we use bind/2:

```
iex>  error_effect_bind = alpha_effect
|> FunPark.Monad.bind(increment_effect)
```

And now, let's run it:

```
iex> FunPark.Monad.Effect.run(error_effect_bind)
%FunPark.Monad.Either.Left{
  left: %ArithmeticError{message: "bad argument in arithmetic expression"}
}
```

We get Either.Left—our increment/1 has produced a failure, but it's an expected I/O error, captured as part of the computation's intended outcome.

I/O typically takes time, so let's simulate this with a half-second delay:

```
iex> delay = fn value -> Process.sleep(500); value end
```

Now map it to to our six_effect/0:

```
iex> long_six_effect = six_effect |> FunPark.Monad.map(delay)
%FunPark.Monad.Effect.Right{
  effect: #Function<...>
}
```

Here, long_six_effect/0 is composed of the directions for three effects: create the number 40, add one, and wait for half a second.

Let's run it in our protected boundary:

```
iex> FunPark.Monad.Effect.run(long_six_effect)
Task completed in 0ms
Task completed in 1ms
Task completed in 502ms
%FunPark.Monad.Either.Right{right: 6}
```

We get Right(41), but now it takes about a half second.

> After a Task runs, it's gone—you can't do anything with it. An Effect, on the other hand, is a description, and descriptions persist.

# Effectful Store

Our Ride expert points out that our current model of ride status is flawed. Right now, it's a Boolean field in the Ride struct—but a ride can be offline for four very different reasons: scheduled maintenance, unscheduled maintenance, a compliance hold, or a fault-triggered lockout.

We need to track the current state in a maintenance database, separating these categories into distinct tables and giving us visibility into *why* a ride is offline.

Earlier, we built A Store for FunPark, on page 170, which lifted Erlang's ETS database into the Either context. We can build on that logic to create an effectful maintenance store, simulating I/O.

To move from Either to an Effect, we need to lift it, but since Either is eager and Effect is lazy, lift_either/1 cannot just take an Either, it needs a thunk that returns an Either.

```
lib/fun_park/maintenance/store.ex
def add(%Ride{} = ride, table) do
  Effect.lift_either(fn -> Store.insert_item(table, ride) end)
  |> map(&simulate_delay/1)
  |> Effect.map_left(&simulate_delay/1)
end
```

add/2 lifts our store's insert_item/2 into an Effect and applies a half-second delay to both the success and error branches. (The code is on the next page.)

lib/fun_park/maintenance/store.ex
```
def get(%Ride{id: id}, table) do
  Effect.lift_either(fn -> Store.get_item(table, id) end)
  |> map(&simulate_delay/1)
  |> Effect.map_left(&simulate_delay/1)
end
```

get/2 takes a Ride, extracts its id, and passes it to get_item/2. As before, we lift the result into an Effect and apply a half-second delay to both branches.

lib/fun_park/maintenance/store.ex
```
def remove(%Ride{id: id}, table) do
  Effect.lift_either(fn -> Store.delete_item(table, id) end)
  |> map(&simulate_delay/1)
  |> Effect.map_left(&simulate_delay/1)
end
```

Similarly, remove/2 deletes a Ride by extracting its id and passing it to delete_item/2.

Together, these form our effectful maintenance store.

## Run It

Let's start by adding a :schedule table to our ETS store:

```
FunPark.Store.create_table(:schedule)
%FunPark.Monad.Either.Right{right: :schedule}
```

Then generate the Apple Cart ride:

```
apple = FunPark.Ride.make("Apple Cart")
%FunPark.Ride{name: "Apple Cart", ...}
```

And create the effects for managing the Apple Cart:

```
save_effect = FunPark.Maintenance.Store.add(apple, :schedule)
get_effect = FunPark.Maintenance.Store.get(apple, :schedule)
remove_effect = FunPark.Maintenance.Store.remove(apple, :schedule)
```

We can run the save Effect:

```
iex> FunPark.Monad.Effect.run(save_effect)
%FunPark.Monad.Either.Right{
  right: %FunPark.Ride{name: "Apple Cart", ... }
}
```

The Effect takes about half a second and returns a Right, indicating the ride was successfully saved.

Say we ask the store for Apple Cart:

```
iex> FunPark.Monad.Effect.run(get_effect)
%FunPark.Monad.Either.Right{
  right: %FunPark.Ride{name: "Apple Cart", ... }
}
```

Again, we get Right in about a half second, expressing success.

Now, let's remove Apple Cart:

```
iex> FunPark.Monad.Effect.run(remove_effect)
%FunPark.Monad.Either.Right{right: 7}
```

Right notes the ride with ID 7 was successfully removed.

Then let's rerun the get_effect/0:

```
iex> FunPark.Monad.Effect.run(get_effect)
%FunPark.Monad.Either.Left{left: :not_found}
```

We get a Left—our I/O lookup failed with a :not_found message.

We can also drop the entire table:

```
FunPark.Store.drop_table(:schedule)
%FunPark.Monad.Either.Right{right: :schedule}
```

Let's run the get Effect again:

```
iex> FunPark.Monad.Effect.run(get_effect)
%FunPark.Monad.Either.Left{
  left: %ArgumentError{...}
}
```

Now the Left contains an ArgumentError—again the I/O failed, but this time for a different reason.

Now that we have an effectful store, we need a repository to hide persistence details and protect the integrity of our domain.

## Maintenance Repository

Earlier, we created a Ride Repository, on page 172. Now let's create a repository for our maintenance service.

## Generate Tables

First we need a quick way to generate all our DB tables.

lib/fun_park/maintenance/repo.ex
```
def create_store do
  Either.sequence_a([
    Store.create_table(:schedule),
    Store.create_table(:unschedule),
    Store.create_table(:lockout),
    Store.create_table(:compliance)
  ])
end
```

Creating a table in ETS can fail, and our Store explicitly manages this failure with the Either monad. With sequence_a/1, each call to the table is evaluated independently, and the results are collected into a single Either—Right(list_of_tables) or Left(list_of_errors).

## Run It

Success is represented by Right with the list of successfully created tables:

```
iex> FunPark.Maintenance.Repo.create_store()
%FunPark.Monad.Either.Right{
  right: [:schedule, :unschedule, :lockout, :compliance]
}
```

But let's run it again:

```
iex> FunPark.Maintenance.Repo.create_store()
%FunPark.Monad.Either.Left{
  left: [
    %ArgumentError{ ... }
    %ArgumentError{ ... }
    %ArgumentError{ ... }
    %ArgumentError{ ... }
  ]
}
```

We get a Left with a list of errors—each one letting us know ETS couldn't create the table, not because it's broken but because it already exists.

## Save a Ride

To save a ride, first we need to validate:

```
lib/fun_park/maintenance/repo.ex
defp validate_ride_effect(ride) do
  Effect.lift_either(fn -> Ride.validate(ride) end)
end
```

Here, we take a Ride and return EffectValidRide.

And we need an Effect to add to the store:

```
lib/fun_park/maintenance/repo.ex
defp add_to_store_effect(valid_ride) do
  Effect.asks(fn env -> env[:table] end)
  |> bind(fn table -> Store.add(valid_ride, table) end)
end
```

This takes a Ride and returns EffectSavedRide using asks/1 to retrieve the table from the environment.

And now that we have Kleisli functions, we can bind them:

```
lib/fun_park/maintenance/repo.ex
def add_ride_effect(%Ride{} = ride) do
  validate_ride_effect(ride)
  |> bind(&add_to_store_effect/1)
end
```

Our repo now protects itself from an invalid Ride before saving to the store.

### Run It

Let's start by creating our store and making a ride:

```
iex> FunPark.Maintenance.Repo.create_store()
iex> apple = FunPark.Ride.make("Apple Cart")
```

Next, create an Effect to add the Apple Cart to scheduled maintenance:

```
iex> effect = FunPark.Maintenance.Repo.add_ride_effect(apple)
%FunPark.Monad.Effect.Right{
  effect: #Function<...>
}
```

And finally execute our Effect with the table name.

```
iex> FunPark.Monad.Effect.run(effect, %{table: :schedule})
Task completed in 0ms
Task completed in 0ms
Task completed in 0ms
Task completed in 501ms
Task completed in 501ms
Task completed in 503ms
```

```
%FunPark.Monad.Either.Right{
  right: %FunPark.Ride{ name: "Apple Cart", ... }
}
```

This involves six tasks. This may look expensive, but these are lightweight BEAM processes, which are far cheaper than most threads. Our challenge in Elixir usually isn't the number of tasks but, rather, how to coordinate them.

Let's save this logic to our repo: add_schedule/1 executes the Effect and provides the environment—in this case, the :schedule table.

lib/fun_park/maintenance/repo.ex
```
def add_schedule(%Ride{} = ride) do
  ride
  |> add_ride_effect()
  |> Effect.run(%{table: :schedule})
end
```

**Run It**

Let's modify the Apple Cart with an invalid wait time:

```
invalid_apple = FunPark.Ride.change(apple, %{wait_time: -10})
```

Now, we'll try to save it:

```
iex> FunPark.Maintenance.Repo.add_schedule(invalid_apple)
%FunPark.Monad.Either.Left{
  left: %FunPark.Errors.ValidationError{
    errors: ["Apple Cart wait time must be non negative"]
  }
}
```

We get Either.Left. The Effect ran but failed with a ValidationError. It short-circuited on validation and did not try to save to the store.

Let's delete the underlying table:

```
FunPark.Store.drop_table(:schedule)
```

And pass it a valid ride:

```
iex> FunPark.Maintenance.Repo.add_schedule(apple)
%FunPark.Monad.Either.Left{
  left: %ArgumentError{
    message: "...does not refer to an existing ETS table..."
  }
}
```

Again, we receive an Either.Left—but this time it contains an ArgumentError, indicating a problem in our store.

An Effect gives the caller structured information about *why* it failed, allowing them to decide how to proceed.

## Save to All

To save our ride to every table, we first need to implement the rest of our maintenance table logic:

lib/fun_park/maintenance/repo.ex
```
def add_unschedule(%Ride{} = ride) do
  ride
  |> add_ride_effect()
  |> Effect.run(%{table: :unschedule})
end

def add_lockout(%Ride{} = ride) do
  ride
  |> add_ride_effect()
  |> Effect.run(%{table: :lockout})
end

def add_compliance(%Ride{} = ride) do
  ride
  |> add_ride_effect()
  |> Effect.run(%{table: :compliance})
end
```

And then bind those Kleisli functions:

lib/fun_park/maintenance.ex
```
def add_to_all(%Ride{} = ride) do
  ride
  |> Repo.add_schedule()
  |> bind(&Repo.add_unschedule/1)
  |> bind(&Repo.add_lockout/1)
  |> bind(&Repo.add_compliance/1)
end
```

Again, with bind/2, the pipeline will short-circuit on the first failure.

Take a minute—what context are we running here?

Each of those add functions runs the Effect. That means we're not binding within the Effect context; we're binding within the Either context. And Either, by definition, is sequential. If we wanted parallelism, we've painted ourself into a corner.

### Run It

Let's start by generating a ride and making sure the store has all the tables:

```
iex> apple = FunPark.Ride.make("Apple Cart")
iex> FunPark.Maintenance.Repo.create_store()
```

Remember, it doesn't matter if create_store/0 returns a Left—that just means the tables already exist.

Now we can add our ride to all the maintenance tables:

```
iex> FunPark.Maintenance.add_to_all(apple)
%FunPark.Monad.Either.Right{
  right: %FunPark.Ride{ name: "Apple Cart", ... }
}
```

The response is a Right, indicating that Apple Cart was successfully saved to all maintenance tables.

Behind the scenes, this call spawned 24 tasks and took about two seconds to complete—our store is pretty pokey, and those four sequential calls are beginning to add up.

> In the BEAM, 24 tasks are trivial to manage, but they're not free. Task setup adds some overhead, about one to three milliseconds in total here. For operations involving I/O, such as database access, that cost is negligible. But in latency-critical domains—like high-frequency trading—even small overheads can matter.

### Remove from All

We also need the ability to remove a ride from our maintenance tables:

```
lib/fun_park/maintenance/repo.ex
defp remove_from_store_effect(valid_ride) do
  Effect.asks(fn env -> env[:table] end)
  |> bind(fn table -> Store.remove(valid_ride, table) end)
end
```

We can compose it with the validation effect:

```
lib/fun_park/maintenance/repo.ex
def remove_ride_effect(%Ride{} = ride) do
  validate_ride_effect(ride)
  |> bind(&remove_from_store_effect/1)
  |> map(fn _ -> ride end)
end
```

This mirrors the add logic: it begins with a Ride, validates it at the boundary, and deletes the ride from the appropriate table. On success, it returns the original Ride, allowing the pipeline to continue.

Next, we need to execute the Effect for each table:

lib/fun_park/maintenance/repo.ex
```elixir
def remove_schedule(%Ride{} = ride) do
  ride
  |> remove_ride_effect()
  |> Effect.run(%{table: :schedule})
end

def remove_unschedule(%Ride{} = ride) do
  ride
  |> remove_ride_effect()
  |> Effect.run(%{table: :unschedule})
end

def remove_lockout(%Ride{} = ride) do
  ride
  |> remove_ride_effect()
  |> Effect.run(%{table: :lockout})
end

def remove_compliance(%Ride{} = ride) do
  ride
  |> remove_ride_effect()
  |> Effect.run(%{table: :compliance})
end
```

Earlier, we used bind/2 to chain the Either results, short-circuiting on the first failure. But these operations are independent—they don't rely on each other's output. Instead of binding, we can use an applicative sequence.

lib/fun_park/maintenance.ex
```elixir
def remove_from_all(%Ride{} = ride) do
  Either.sequence_a([
    Repo.remove_schedule(ride),
    Repo.remove_unschedule(ride),
    Repo.remove_lockout(ride),
    Repo.remove_compliance(ride)
  ])
  |> map(fn _ -> ride end)
end
```

Here, like validation, on success we map back to the original Ride. The result is either a success or a list of failures.

**Run It**

First, let's create our store and make an Apple Cart ride:

```
iex> FunPark.Maintenance.Repo.create_store()
iex> apple = FunPark.Ride.make("Apple Cart")
```

We can add the Apple Cart to all maintenance tables:

```
iex> FunPark.Maintenance.add_to_all(apple)
%FunPark.Monad.Either.Right{
  right: %FunPark.Ride{ name: "Apple Cart", ... }
}
```

We can remove it as well:

```
iex> FunPark.Maintenance.remove_from_all(apple)
%FunPark.Monad.Either.Right{
  right: %FunPark.Ride{ name: "Apple Cart", ... }
}
```

On success, it doesn't matter whether we used bind/2 or sequence_a/1—both approaches yield the same result.

But say we create an invalid Apple Cart:

```
iex> invalid_apple = FunPark.Ride.change(apple, %{wait_time: -10})
```

The difference matters—adding Apple Cart to all our tables will stop at the first error:

```
iex> FunPark.Maintenance.add_to_all(invalid_apple)
%FunPark.Monad.Either.Left{
  left: %FunPark.Errors.ValidationError{
    errors: ["Apple Cart wait time must be non negative"]
  }
}
```

But removing it will attempt *all* removals independently, returning a *list* of validation errors:

```
iex> FunPark.Maintenance.remove_from_all(invalid_apple)
%FunPark.Monad.Either.Left{
  left: %FunPark.Errors.ValidationError{
    errors: [
      "Apple Cart wait time must be non negative",
      "Apple Cart wait time must be non negative",
      "Apple Cart wait time must be non negative",
      "Apple Cart wait time must be non negative"
```

```
    ]
  }
}
```

Now let's try a valid ride with a broken store:

```
iex> FunPark.Store.drop_table(:schedule)
```

With add_to_all/1, the internal bind/2 will halt on the first error:

```
iex> FunPark.Maintenance.add_to_all(apple)
%FunPark.Monad.Either.Left{
  left: %ArgumentError{
    message: "...no existing ETS table..."
  }
}
```

But remove_from_all/1 uses sequence_a/1 and will independently run all removal effects:

```
iex> FunPark.Maintenance.remove_from_all(apple)
%FunPark.Monad.Either.Left{
  left: [
    %ArgumentError{
      message: "... no existing ETS table ..."
    }
  ]
}
```

Here, we still have a list but only one ArgumentError, telling us one Effect failed. We can deduce the rest succeeded.

Sometimes we want to stop at the first error, especially when continuing doesn't make sense. Other times, a best-effort approach is more appropriate—where we want to try everything and report the results. It depends on the problem. Is failure unrecoverable, making later steps irrelevant? Is each step expensive, so we want to avoid unnecessary work? Then use bind/2. If steps can run independently—and failure in one doesn't affect the others—sequence_a/1 lets us try them all.

## Inject Behavior, Not Configuration

Let's take another look at add_ride_effect/1:

```
lib/fun_park/maintenance/repo.ex
def add_ride_effect(%Ride{} = ride) do
  validate_ride_effect(ride)
  |> bind(&add_to_store_effect/1)
end
```

> ### Joe asks:
> ### Which Is Faster?
>
> On failure, bind/2 with its short-circuiting will be faster than sequence_a/1, which always runs all effects. On success, it's a bit of a trick question. Independence sounds like concurrency, so it's easy to assume that sequence_a/1 runs faster than bind/2. But that confuses structure with execution. Applicative sequencing guarantees structural independence—steps don't depend on each other—but it says nothing about *when* or *how* they run.

Configuration is injected (env[:table]), but the use of Store.add/2 embeds a specific store implementation, creating tight coupling and limiting flexibility.

Let's fix this in our has_ride_effect/1:

```
lib/fun_park/maintenance/repo.ex
def has_ride_effect(%Ride{} = ride, table) do
  Effect.asks(fn env -> env[:store] end)
  |> bind(fn store -> store.get(ride, table) end)
  |> map(fn _ -> ride end)
end
```

Here, the function knows it needs to call store.get/2, but it doesn't know which store is being used. We're not injecting a configuration, we're injecting behavior.

Unlike add_ride_effect/1, our has_ride_effect/2 is loosely coupled, making it easy to swap between dev and prod environments. More importantly, it enables evolutionary design: we can confidently defer architectural decisions and continue using this simple store until the domain demands something more sophisticated.

Next, we need our table-specific checks.

```
lib/fun_park/maintenance/repo.ex
def in_schedule(%Ride{} = ride), do: has_ride_effect(ride, :schedule)
def in_unschedule(%Ride{} = ride), do: has_ride_effect(ride, :unschedule)
def in_lockout(%Ride{} = ride), do: has_ride_effect(ride, :lockout)
def in_compliance(%Ride{} = ride), do: has_ride_effect(ride, :compliance)
```

These check whether a ride is present in a specific maintenance table. Notice the absence of run/2—unlike our add and remove logic, these functions remain in the Effect context, not Either.

## Run It

Again, let's create the store and make an Apple Cart ride:

```
FunPark.Maintenance.Repo.create_store()
apple = FunPark.Ride.make("Apple Cart")
```

Next, generate an Effect to check if it's in scheduled maintenance:

```
effect = FunPark.Maintenance.Repo.in_schedule(apple)
```

And create the environment with our Store:

```
env = %{store: FunPark.Maintenance.Store}
```

Let's run the Effect in the environment:

```
FunPark.Monad.Effect.run(effect, env)
%FunPark.Monad.Either.Left{left: :not_found}
```

The response is Left, indicating failure, with the :not_found message.

But let's add Apple Cart to scheduled maintenance:

```
FunPark.Maintenance.Repo.add_schedule(apple)
%FunPark.Monad.Either.Right{
  right: %FunPark.Ride{name: "Apple Cart", ... }
}
```

Then let's rerun our Effect:

```
FunPark.Monad.Effect.run(effect, env)
Task completed in 501ms
%FunPark.Monad.Either.Right{
  right: %FunPark.Ride{name: "Apple Cart", ... }
}
```

Apple Cart is now in scheduled maintenance.

We can further compose the effects to discover whether a ride is in all maintenance tables:

```
lib/fun_park/maintenance.ex
def check_in_all(%Ride{} = ride) do
  ride
  |> Repo.in_schedule()
  |> bind(&Repo.in_unschedule/1)
  |> bind(&Repo.in_lockout/1)
  |> bind(&Repo.in_compliance/1)
  |> Effect.run(%{store: Store})
end
```

Checking whether a Ride is present in all four maintenance tables is a matter of chaining the Effect Kleisli functions with bind/2 and running the combined Effect in an environment with the Store.

If the ride is found in all tables, we get a Right; if any check fails, the sequence short-circuits and returns a Left.

## Run It

We start by creating our store and generating a new ride:

```
FunPark.Maintenance.Repo.create_store()
apple = FunPark.Ride.make("Apple Cart")
```

Since nothing has been added yet, check_in_all/1 fails with a Left:

```
FunPark.Maintenance.check_in_all(apple)
%FunPark.Monad.Either.Left{left: :not_found}
```

In half a second, it returns :not_found.

Say we add the ride to all four maintenance tables:

```
iex> FunPark.Maintenance.add_to_all(apple)
%FunPark.Monad.Either.Right{
  right: %FunPark.Ride{ name: "Apple Cart", ... }
}
```

We then rerun check_in_all/1:

```
FunPark.Maintenance.check_in_all(apple)
%FunPark.Monad.Either.Right{
  right: %FunPark.Ride{ name: "Apple Cart", ... }
}
```

It succeeds, but takes two seconds.

We remove it from our :lockout table:

```
FunPark.Maintenance.Repo.remove_lockout(apple)
%FunPark.Monad.Either.Right{
  right: %FunPark.Ride{name: "Apple Cart", ... }
}
```

Once again, we run our check_in_all/1:

```
FunPark.Maintenance.check_in_all(apple)
%FunPark.Monad.Either.Left{left: :not_found}
```

It fails, but only after iterating though three tables, taking one and a half seconds.

## Flip the Logic

Our Ride expert reminds us: a ride is considered online only when it is *not* in scheduled or unscheduled maintenance, *not* locked out, and *not* under compliance review. While we have logic to confirm when a Ride appears in *every* table, what we need now is the opposite—a ride is online when it is *absent* from *all* tables.

Earlier, in remove_from_all/1, we used sequence_a/1, which returns a Right when all succeed or a Left containing a list of failures. We could apply the same strategy in check_in_all/1, inferring that a ride is online by counting the number of failures: if all four checks fail, the ride is absent from all tables. But this approach is brittle—it depends on knowing there are exactly four maintenance tables. When the domain evolves, that logic breaks. Instead, we need something more general.

Our first problem is the bias: Either is biased toward the Right, but in our current implementation a Right means the value was found. What we need is the opposite—a Right should mean the value was *not* found. So before we can sequence, we need to flip the logic.

Let's start with the Effect:

```
lib/fun_park/maintenance/repo.ex
def assert_absent_effect(%Ride{} = ride, kleisli_fn, reason_msg) do
  ride
  |> kleisli_fn.()
  |> Effect.flip_either()
  |> bind(right_if_absent(ride))
  |> Effect.map_left(replace_ride_with_reason(reason_msg))
end

defp right_if_absent(ride) do
  fn
    :not_found -> Effect.right(ride)
    other -> Effect.left(other)
  end
end

defp replace_ride_with_reason(reason_msg) do
  fn
    %Ride{} -> reason_msg
    other -> other
  end
end
```

Here, we call the Kleisli function to check a maintenance table, then use flip_either/1 to invert our Right and Left, putting failures on the Right. Next, we call right_if_absent/1, which includes branching logic, plucking the :not_found case and returning Right(ride) and passing other errors back to the Left. Finally, we need to clean up the Left side with replace_ride_with_reason/1: if the failure is that the Ride *was* found, return a human-readable message; otherwise, just pass the unknown error through unchanged.

Our success is now when a Ride is absent!

```
lib/fun_park/maintenance/repo.ex
def not_in_schedule(%Ride{} = ride) do
  assert_absent_effect(
    ride,
    &in_schedule/1,
    "#{ride.name} is in scheduled maintenance"
  )
end

def not_in_unschedule(%Ride{} = ride) do
  assert_absent_effect(
    ride,
    &in_unschedule/1,
    "#{ride.name} is in unscheduled maintenance"
  )
end

def not_in_lockout(%Ride{} = ride) do
  assert_absent_effect(
    ride,
    &in_lockout/1,
    "#{ride.name} is locked out"
  )
end

def not_in_compliance(%Ride{} = ride) do
  assert_absent_effect(
    ride,
    &in_compliance/1,
    "#{ride.name} is out of compliance"
  )
end
```

And we bind them to check that a ride is *not* in any scheduled maintenance.

```
lib/fun_park/maintenance.ex
def check_online_bind(%Ride{} = ride) do
  ride
  |> Repo.not_in_schedule()
  |> bind(&Repo.not_in_unschedule/1)
  |> bind(&Repo.not_in_lockout/1)
```

```
  |> bind(&Repo.not_in_compliance/1)
  |> Effect.run(%{store: Store})
end
```

Here, check_online_bind/1 creates a structure where computations are concurrent but the control flow is sequential. Each check runs in its own process, but the next step starts only if the previous returns a Right. Since each check takes approximately half a second, the best-case scenario is when the first check fails, ending the chain in 0.5 seconds. The worst case occurs when all checks succeed, resulting in a cumulative runtime of 2 seconds.

## Run It

Again, start by creating the store and a ride:

```
FunPark.Maintenance.Repo.create_store()
apple = FunPark.Ride.make("Apple Cart")
```

And let's clean up the store to be certain Apple Cart is not saved:

```
iex> FunPark.Maintenance.remove_from_all(apple)
```

Then check whether it's online:

```
FunPark.Maintenance.check_online_bind(apple)
Task completed in 502ms
Task completed in 1003ms
Task completed in 1504ms
Task completed in 2006ms
%FunPark.Monad.Either.Right{
  right: %FunPark.Ride{name: "Apple Cart", ... }
}
```

Because it's not present in any maintenance table, the check runs all four steps and succeeds—taking about two seconds in total.

Now let's add it back to *all* the tables:

```
iex> FunPark.Maintenance.add_to_all(apple)
```

When we run the check again, we get an answer in just half a second:

```
iex> FunPark.Maintenance.check_online_bind(apple)
FunPark.Maintenance.check_online_bind(apple)
%FunPark.Monad.Either.Left{left: "Apple Cart is in schedule maintenance"}
```

Short-circuiting means we stopped on the first error, never reaching for the other checks.

Implementing this updated logic is just a matter of replacing a couple of our functions. Let's start with our online?/1:

lib/fun_park/ride.ex
```
def online?(%__MODULE__{online: online}), do: online
```

Here we're checking the online key in the Ride struct. We can swap it out with our updated logic:

lib/fun_park/maintenance.ex
```
def online?(%Ride{} = ride) do
  ride
  |> check_online()
  |> Either.right?()
end
```

Here we run our maintenance checks with the Either.right?/1 refinement, which transforms our Right or Left to the predicate's true or false.

Next, let's look at our ensure_online validation:

lib/fun_park/ride.ex
```
def ensure_online(%__MODULE__{} = ride) do
  Either.lift_predicate(
    ride,
    &online?/1,
    fn r -> "#{r.name} is offline" end
  )
  |> Either.map_left(&ValidationError.new/1)
end
```

We could stick with this if we're happy with our simple offline message, but if we need to propagate the messages from check_online/1, we call check_online/1 directly and wrap the Left results in a ValidationError.

lib/fun_park/maintenance.ex
```
def ensure_online(%Ride{} = ride) do
  ride
  |> check_online()
  |> Either.map_left(&ValidationError.new/1)
end
```

That's it—with just two small changes our system is now checking the maintenance system to determine a ride's online status.

### All Major Theme Parks Have Delays

The Ride expert has flagged a sharp uptick in complaints: sluggish behavior, unpredictable delays, guest experiences falling apart. The culprit is clear: our slow maintenance I/O is clogging the system. While our solution technically works, it doesn't hold up under load. Caching might help, but in this case, any outdated information poses a safety risk.

Fortunately, the checks are independent—they don't share state or rely on each other's results. This means we can use applicative sequencing in the Effect context to run them in parallel.

```
lib/fun_park/maintenance.ex
def check_online(%Ride{} = ride) do
  Effect.validate(ride, [
    &Repo.not_in_schedule/1,
    &Repo.not_in_unschedule/1,
    &Repo.not_in_lockout/1,
    &Repo.not_in_compliance/1
  ])
  |> Effect.run(%{store: Store})
end
```

Here, we treat our checks as a validation problem: take an input, apply multiple independent checks, and return the original value—but within the Effect context.

| Operation | Description | Either | Effect |
|---|---|---|---|
| bind | Chain computations | Sequential | Sequential |
| traverse/2 | Monadic sequence | Sequential | Sequential |
| traverse_a/2 | Applicative sequence | Sequential | Parallel |

### Run It

Let's clean up by removing Apple Cart from every table:

```
FunPark.Maintenance.remove_from_all(apple)
```

And check whether it's online:

```
FunPark.Maintenance.check_online(apple)
%FunPark.Monad.Either.Right{
  right: %FunPark.Ride{name: "Apple Cart", ... }
}
```

We still receive that Apple Cart is online. It's not present in any of our maintenance tables. Better yet, it runs all four independent checks concurrently, completing in just half a second.

Let's add it back to *all* the tables:

```
iex> FunPark.Maintenance.add_to_all(apple)
```

Then run the check:

```
FunPark.Maintenance.check_online(apple)
%FunPark.Monad.Either.Left{
  left: %FunPark.Errors.ValidationError{
    errors: ["Apple Cart is out of compliance", "Apple Cart is locked out",
    "Apple Cart is in unscheduled maintenance",
    "Apple Cart is in scheduled maintenance"]
  }
}
```

Again, we get an answer in a half second, but now, instead of short-circuiting on the first failure, we receive a full list.

After further discussions with our Ride expert, we discover additional information: a Patron who isn't eligible to ride doesn't need to know whether the ride is online. That lets us trim additional time by only checking online status for those who are eligible.

```
lib/fun_park/ride/fast_lane.ex
def validate_fast_pass_lane_b(%Patron{} = patron, %Ride{} = ride) do
  validate_vip_or_pass = curry(&ensure_vip_or_fast_pass/2)
  validate_eligibility = curry(&validate_eligibility/2)

  Either.validate(
    ride,
    [
      validate_eligibility.(patron),
      validate_vip_or_pass.(patron)
    ]
  )
  |> bind(&Maintenance.ensure_online/1)
  |> map(fn _ -> patron end)
end
```

Our original validate_fast_pass_lane/2 applied all checks up front, including ensure_online/1. In contrast, validate_fast_pass_lane_b/2 uses bind/2 to separate the Patron eligibility from the Ride availability, only applying the expensive maintenance lookups for eligible patrons.

## Run It

First, let's make sure our store is created and then generate a couple of patrons and a ride.

```
FunPark.Maintenance.Repo.create_store()
iex> beth = FunPark.Patron.make( "Beth", 16, 115)
iex> elsie = FunPark.Patron.make( "Elsie", 17, 135, ticket_tier: :vip)

iex> haunted_mansion = FunPark.Ride.make(
  "Haunted Mansion",
  min_age: 14,
  min_height: 120
)
```

Now check if Beth can enter the FastPass lane:

```
iex> FunPark.Ride.FastLane.validate_fast_pass_lane_b(beth, haunted_mansion)
%FunPark.Monad.Either.Left{
  left: %FunPark.Errors.ValidationError{
    errors: ["Beth is not tall enough", "Beth does not have a fast pass"]
  }
}
```

No, she can't, but because she's ineligible, this call took a millisecond.

Let's check Elsie:

```
iex> FunPark.Ride.FastLane.validate_fast_pass_lane_b(elsie, haunted_mansion)
%FunPark.Monad.Either.Right{
  right: %FunPark.Patron{ name: "Elsie", ... }
}
```

Elsie is eligible, so the call takes a half second to check if the Haunted Mansion is online.

Later, the Haunted Mansion throws a fault and triggers a lockout.

```
iex> FunPark.Maintenance.Repo.add_lockout(haunted_mansion)
```

Now, we check Elsie again:

```
iex> FunPark.Ride.FastLane.validate_fast_pass_lane_b(elsie, haunted_mansion)
%FunPark.Monad.Either.Left{
  left: %FunPark.Errors.ValidationError{
    errors: ["Haunted Mansion is locked out"]
  }
}
```

Again the call takes a half second but determines that although she is eligible, Elsie can't enter the fast lane because the Haunted Mansion is in a safety lockout.

Effect is well suited for async validation, data augmentation, and coordinating external checks. But if your system requires streaming, pipelines, backpressure, or distributed coordination, see *Concurrent Data Processing in Elixir [Gos21]* by Svilen Gospodinov or *Network Programming in Elixir and Erlang [Leo25]* by Andrea Leopardi.

## What You've Learned

In this chapter, we covered how to model effectful code as instructions—deferring execution to a controlled boundary. We turned Elixir's eager Task into a lazy Effect, and reused familiar tools—map, bind, traverse, and sequence—in a new context. Along the way, we uncovered something unexpected: parallelism.

As we wrap things up, think back to the first time you saw functional code:

> *"How the heck am I supposed to understand this? It's just a bunch of maps and binds!"*

Imperative code lays everything out step by step. It might be harder to maintain, but at least it feels familiar.

But familiarity can hold us back. It's easy to fall into habits, patching loops and conditionals without rethinking how we model logic. The code changes, but the thinking stays the same.

It's like chess. Playing more games doesn't make you better—structure and feedback do. Masters don't think in moves; they think in patterns. They see the board as a system: repeatable, predictable, and composable.

Functional programming offers a similar shift. It gives you tools to compose logic in smaller, more stable units—shaping not just how you code but how you think.

That shift takes practice. Mastery doesn't come from watching or repeating—it comes from building, experimenting, and reflecting. Don't just run the FunPark examples. Try variations. Build your own. Break things and fix them. That's how understanding deepens—not all at once, but step by step.

This book can't do the work for you, but it can help light the path—showing what to practice, in what order, and why it matters. It can help you focus your attention, avoid common missteps, and move forward with purpose.

# CHAPTER 11

# Answers

## Equality Chapter Answers

### Normalize Strings

Elixir considers these strings unequal:

```
iex> string_1 = "Alice"
iex> string_2 = " alice "

iex> string_1 == string_2
false
```

And by default, our Eq falls back to Elixir's logic:

```
iex> FunPark.Eq.Utils.eq?(string_1, string_2)
false
```

But we can change the behavior by normalizing the strings *before* they enter the comparison:

```
iex> normalize = fn s -> s |> String.trim() |> String.downcase() end
iex> eq_normalized = FunPark.Eq.Utils.contramap(normalize)
```

And now we know these strings, when normalized, are equal:

```
iex> FunPark.Eq.Utils.eq?(string_1, string_2, eq_normalized)
true
```

### Transferring Passes

Start by generating a few rides and FastPasses:

```
iex> tea_cup = FunPark.Ride.make("Tea Cup")
iex> haunted_mansion = FunPark.Ride.make("Haunted Mansion")
iex> ghost_hollow = FunPark.Ride.make("Ghost Hollow")
iex> jungle_river = FunPark.Ride.make("Jungle River")
```

```
iex> datetime_a = DateTime.new!(~D[2025-06-01], ~T[13:00:00])
iex> datetime_b = DateTime.new!(~D[2025-06-01], ~T[13:30:00])
iex> datetime_c = DateTime.new!(~D[2025-06-01], ~T[14:00:00])

iex> pass_a = FunPark.FastPass.make(tea_cup, datetime_a)
iex> pass_b = FunPark.FastPass.make(haunted_mansion, datetime_b)
iex> pass_c = FunPark.FastPass.make(ghost_hollow, datetime_c)
iex> pass_d = FunPark.FastPass.make(jungle_river, datetime_a)
```

Now give Alice and Beth each a list of FastPasses:

```
iex> alice = [pass_a, pass_b]
iex> beth = [pass_c, pass_d]
```

If we check for duplicates using the default Eq, there's no overlap:

```
iex> FunPark.List.intersection(alice, beth)
[]
```

But if we define equality based on time, we see they have passes for the same time:

```
iex> has_eq_time = FunPark.FastPass.eq_time()
iex> FunPark.List.intersection(alice, beth, has_eq_time)
[
  %FunPark.FastPass{
    id: 4322,
    ride: %FunPark.Ride{
      name: "Tea Cup",
      ...
    },
    time: ~U[2025-06-01 13:00:00Z]
  }
]
```

By changing the definition of equality, we can see that a simple transfer of passes from Alice to Beth isn't safe—there's a conflict in the schedule.

# Order Chapter Answers

### Patron Ord by Reward Points

Within the FunPark.Patron module:

```
lib/fun_park/patron.ex
def get_reward_points(%__MODULE__{reward_points: reward_points}),
  do: reward_points

def ord_by_reward_points do
  Ord.Utils.contramap(&get_reward_points/1)
end
```

## Ride Ord by Wait Time

Within the FunPark.Ride module:

lib/fun_park/ride.ex
```
def get_wait_time(%__MODULE__{wait_time: wait_time}), do: wait_time

def ord_by_wait_time do
  Ord.Utils.contramap(&get_wait_time/1)
end
```

## Eq Macro

Within the FunPark.Macros module:

lib/fun_park/macros.ex
```
defmacro eq_for(for_struct, field) do
  quote do
    alias FunPark.Eq

    defimpl FunPark.Eq, for: unquote(for_struct) do
      def eq?(
            %unquote(for_struct){unquote(field) => v1},
            %unquote(for_struct){unquote(field) => v2}
          ),
          do: Eq.eq?(v1, v2)

      def not_eq?(
            %unquote(for_struct){unquote(field) => v1},
            %unquote(for_struct){unquote(field) => v2}
          ),
          do: Eq.not_eq?(v1, v2)
    end
  end
end
```

## Min and Max

Within the FunPark.Ord.Utils module:

lib/fun_park/ord/utils.ex
```
def min(a, b, ord \\ Ord) do
  case compare(a, b, ord) do
    :gt -> b
    _ -> a
  end
end
```

lib/fun_park/ord/utils.ex
```
def max(a, b, ord \\ Ord) do
  case compare(a, b, ord) do
    :lt -> b
    _ -> a
```

```
    end
end
```

# Monoid Chapter Answers

## Product Monoid

Create a new Monoid.Product module:

lib/fun_park/monoid/product.ex
```elixir
defmodule FunPark.Monoid.Product do
  @type t :: %__MODULE__{value: number()}

  defstruct value: 1
end

defimpl FunPark.Monoid, for: FunPark.Monoid.Product do
  alias FunPark.Monoid.Product

  @spec empty(Product.t()) :: Product.t()
  def empty(_), do: %Product{}

  @spec append(Product.t(), Product.t()) :: Product.t()
  def append(%Product{value: a}, %Product{value: b}) do
    %Product{value: a * b}
  end

  @spec wrap(Product.t(), number()) :: Product.t()
  def wrap(%Product{}, value) when is_number(value),
    do: %Product{value: value}

  @spec unwrap(Product.t()) :: number()
  def unwrap(%Product{value: value}) when is_number(value), do: value
end
```

## Min Monoid

Create a new Monoid.Min module:

lib/fun_park/monoid/min.ex
```elixir
defmodule FunPark.Monoid.Min do
  defstruct value: nil, id: nil, ord: FunPark.Ord
end

defimpl FunPark.Monoid, for: FunPark.Monoid.Min do
  alias FunPark.Monoid.Min
  alias FunPark.Ord.Utils

  def empty(%Min{id: id, ord: ord}), do: %Min{value: id, id: id, ord: ord}

  def append(%Min{value: a, ord: ord} = min1, %Min{value: b}) do
    %Min{min1 | value: Utils.min(a, b, ord)}
  end
```

```
   def wrap(%Min{ord: ord}, value) do
      %Min{value: value, ord: Utils.to_ord_map(ord)}
   end

   def unwrap(%Min{value: value}), do: value
end
```

# Predicate Chapter Answers

## Manage Likes and Dislikes

likes and dislikes need to be mutually exclusive.

lib/fun_park/patron.ex
```
def get_likes(%__MODULE__{likes: likes}), do: likes
def get_dislikes(%__MODULE__{dislikes: dislikes}), do: dislikes

def add_likes(%__MODULE__{} = patron, likes)
    when is_list(likes) do
  updated_likes = List.union(likes, get_likes(patron))
  updated_dislikes = List.difference(get_dislikes(patron), updated_likes)

  change(patron, %{
    likes: updated_likes,
    dislikes: updated_dislikes
  })
end

def remove_likes(%__MODULE__{} = patron, likes)
    when is_list(likes) do
  updated_likes = List.difference(get_likes(patron), likes)
  change(patron, %{likes: updated_likes})
end

def add_dislikes(
      %__MODULE__{} = patron,
      dislikes
    )
    when is_list(dislikes) do
  updated_dislikes = List.union(dislikes, get_dislikes(patron))
  updated_likes = List.difference(get_likes(patron), updated_dislikes)

  change(patron, %{
    dislikes: updated_dislikes,
    likes: updated_likes
  })
end

def remove_dislikes(
      %__MODULE__{} = patron,
      dislikes
    )
    when is_list(dislikes) do
```

```
    updated_dislikes = List.difference(get_dislikes(patron), dislikes)
    change(patron, %{dislikes: updated_dislikes})
end
```

## Add Each Predicate

Define each predicate:

```
lib/fun_park/patron.ex
def likes_ride?(%__MODULE__{likes: likes}, %Ride{} = ride) do
  Ride.has_any_tag?(ride, likes)
end

def dislikes_ride?(%__MODULE__{dislikes: dislikes}, %Ride{} = ride) do
  Ride.has_any_tag?(ride, dislikes)
end
```

## Add Recommended Logic

This composes likes_ride?/2 and the negation of dislikes_ride?/2, along with the function suggested?/2, which itself checks that the patron is eligible, the ride is online, and the wait time is not too long.

```
lib/fun_park/patron.ex
def recommended?(
      %__MODULE__{} = patron,
      %Ride{} = ride
    ) do
  p_all([
    curry(&likes_ride?/2).(patron),
    p_not(curry(&dislikes_ride?/2).(patron)),
    curry(&Ride.suggested?/2).(patron)
  ]).(ride)
end
```

# Maybe Chapter Answers

We define priority_fast_lane/2 to apply ride-specific access rules and return the highest-priority eligible patron:

```
lib/fun_park/ride.ex
def priority_fast_lane(patrons, %__MODULE__{} = ride)
    when is_list(patrons) do
  m_concat(
    Patron.max_priority_maybe_monoid(),
    patrons |> Enum.map(&fast_pass_lane(&1, ride))
  )
end
```

This function maps each patron into the MaybeFastPassPatron context, then folds the results using a max monoid that compares eligible patrons by priority.

Let's start by generating our ride and a FastPass:

```
iex> haunted_mansion = FunPark.Ride.make("Haunted Mansion", min_age: 14)
```

```
iex> datetime = DateTime.new!(~D[2025-06-01], ~T[13:00:00])
iex> fast_pass = FunPark.FastPass.make(haunted_mansion, datetime)
```

The Haunted Mansion requires riders to be at least 14. We also generate a valid FastPass for that ride.

Next, generate our patrons:

```
iex> alice = FunPark.Patron.make(
  "Alice", 15, 120,
  reward_points: 50, ticket_tier: :premium,
  fast_passes: [fast_pass]
)

iex> beth = FunPark.Patron.make(
  "Beth", 16, 130,
  reward_points: 20, ticket_tier: :vip
)

iex> charles = FunPark.Patron.make(
  "Charles", 12, 135,
  reward_points: 150, ticket_tier: :vip
)
```

- Alice has a valid FassPass and meets the age requirement.
- Beth is a VIP and also meets the requirement.
- Charles is a VIP but too young for the ride.

Let's test all three:

```
iex> all_patrons = [alice, beth, charles]
iex> FunPark.Ride.priority_fast_lane(all_patrons, haunted_mansion)
%FunPark.Monad.Maybe.Just{
  value: %FunPark.Patron{
    name: "Beth",
  }
}
```

Beth is selected—she's a VIP and eligible for the ride, and her tier gives her higher priority than Alice.

If we remove Beth, Alice becomes the top candidate:

```
iex> FunPark.Ride.priority_fast_lane([alice, charles], haunted_mansion)
%FunPark.Monad.Maybe.Just{
  value: %FunPark.Patron{
    name: "Alice",
    ...
  }
```

```
}
```

Alice qualifies based on her FastPass and age and is selected when Beth is no longer in the list.

Now try Charles alone:

```
iex> FunPark.Ride.priority_fast_lane([charles], haunted_mansion)
%FunPark.Monad.Maybe.Nothing{}
```

Even though Charles has the most reward points, he's too young for the ride. In the MaybeFastPassPatron context, he's *nothing*.

# Either Chapter Answers

We started with validate_fast_pass_lane/2, which takes a patron and a ride and returns Right(patron) or Left(list_of_reasons):

lib/fun_park/ride/fast_lane.ex
```
def validate_fast_pass_lane(%Patron{} = patron, %Ride{} = ride) do
  validate_eligibility = curry(&validate_eligibility/2)
  validate_vip_or_pass = curry(&ensure_vip_or_fast_pass/2)
  Either.validate(
    ride,
    [
      validate_eligibility.(patron),
      validate_vip_or_pass.(patron),
      &Ride.ensure_online/1
    ]
  )
  |> map(fn _ -> patron end)
end
```

## Single Eligibility Notice

lib/fun_park/ride/fast_lane.ex
```
def validate_answer_a(%Patron{} = patron, %Ride{} = ride) do
  validate_vip_or_pass = curry(&ensure_vip_or_fast_pass/2)

  validate_eligibility =
    curry(fn p, r ->
      validate_eligibility(p, r)
      |> Either.map_left(fn _ ->
        "#{Patron.get_name(p)} is not eligible for this ride"
      end)
    end)

  Either.validate(
    ride,
    [
      validate_eligibility.(patron),
      validate_vip_or_pass.(patron),
```

```
        &Ride.ensure_online/1
      ]
    )
    |> map(fn _ -> patron end)
end
```

Here we introduce a refinement: we no longer care *why* the patron is ineligible, only that they are. So we update the message by piping the result through map_left/2.

## Check Ride Online First

lib/fun_park/ride/fast_lane.ex
```
def validate_answer_b(%Patron{} = patron, %Ride{} = ride) do
  validate_vip_or_pass = curry(&ensure_vip_or_fast_pass/2)
  validate_eligibility = curry(&validate_eligibility/2)

  validate_fast_lane =
    Either.validate(
      ride,
      [
        validate_eligibility.(patron),
        validate_vip_or_pass.(patron)
      ]
    )

  Ride.ensure_online(ride)
  |> Either.map_left(fn message -> [message] end)
  |> ap(validate_fast_lane)
  |> map(fn _ -> patron end)
end
```

Here we check whether the ride is online; if it isn't, we wrap the error in a list to match the validation structure. Then we apply ap/2 to run the eligibility and FastPass validations. Finally, we use map/2 to return the patron if all checks pass.

This gives us our first opportunity to use an applicative. Both the online check and the validations are in the Either context, so we use ap/2 to apply the result of ensure_online/1 to the combined validation logic. If either is Left, the computation short-circuits.

## Create Custom Messages

lib/fun_park/ride/fast_lane.ex
```
def validate_answer_c(%Patron{} = patron, %Ride{} = ride) do
  validate_fast_lane =
    curry_r(fn p, r ->
      ensure_vip_or_fast_pass(p, r)
      |> Either.map_left(fn _ ->
```

```
          "#{Patron.get_name(p)} can ride, but not through the fast lane"
        end)
    end)
  validate_eligibility =
    curry_r(fn p, r ->
      validate_eligibility(p, r)
      |> Either.map_left(fn _ ->
        "#{Patron.get_name(p)} is not eligible for this ride"
      end)
    end)
  Either.validate(
    patron,
    [
      validate_eligibility.(ride),
      validate_fast_lane.(ride)
    ]
  )
  |> map(fn _ ->
    "#{Patron.get_name(patron)} can enter the fast lane"
  end)
  |> Either.map_left(fn [first | _] -> first end)
end
```

In this version, we apply multiple validations, but ordered by relevance to the patron. Eligibility is checked first since it determines whether the patron can ride at all, followed by fast lane access. After the checks, we use map_left/2 to extract the first error.

# Bibliography

[Arm13]    Joe Armstrong. *Programming Erlang (2nd edition)*. The Pragmatic Bookshelf, Dallas, TX, 2nd, 2013.

[Bro95]    Frederick P. Brooks Jr. *The Mythical Man-Month: Essays on Software Engineering*. Addison-Wesley, Boston, MA, Anniversary, 1995.

[EP16]     Anders Ericsson and Robert Pool. *Peak: Secrets from the New Science of Expertise*. Houghton Mifflin Company, New York, NY, 2016.

[Eva03]    Eric Evans. *Domain-Driven Design: Tackling Complexity in the Heart of Software*. Addison-Wesley Longman, Boston, MA, 2003.

[Gos21]    Svilen Gospodinov. *Concurrent Data Processing in Elixir*. The Pragmatic Bookshelf, Dallas, TX, 2021.

[Leo25]    Andrea Leopardi. *Network Programming in Elixir and Erlang*. The Pragmatic Bookshelf, Dallas, TX, 2025.

[Pin09]    Daniel H. Pink. *Drive: The Surprising Truth About What Motivates Us*. Riverhead Books, New York, NY, 2009.

[Sw17]     Michael Swaine and the PragPub writers. *Functional Programming: A PragPub Anthology*. The Pragmatic Bookshelf, Dallas, TX, 2017.

[Tho18]    Dave Thomas. *Programming Elixir 1.6*. The Pragmatic Bookshelf, Dallas, TX, 2018.

[Wla18]    Scott Wlaschin. *Domain Modeling Made Functional*. The Pragmatic Bookshelf, Dallas, TX, 2018.

[WM19]     Darin Wilson and Eric Meadows-Jönsson. *Programming Ecto*. The Pragmatic Bookshelf, Dallas, TX, 2019.

# Thank you!

We hope you enjoyed this book and that you're already thinking about what you want to learn next. To help make that decision easier, we're offering you this gift.

Head on over to https://pragprog.com right now, and use the coupon code BUYANOTHER2025 to save 30% on your next ebook. Offer is void where prohibited or restricted. This offer does not apply to any edition of *The Pragmatic Programmer* ebook.

And if you'd like to share your own expertise with the world, why not propose a writing idea to us? After all, many of our best authors started off as our readers, just like you. With up to a 50% royalty, world-class editorial services, and a name you trust, there's nothing to lose. Visit https://pragprog.com/become-an-author/ today to learn more and to get started.

Thank you for your continued support. We hope to hear from you again soon!

The Pragmatic Bookshelf

# From Ruby to Elixir

Elixir will change the way you think about programming. Use your Ruby experience to quickly get up to speed so you can see what all of the buzz is about. Go from zero to production applications that are reliable, fast, and scalable. Learn Elixir syntax and pattern matching to conquer the basics. Then move onto Elixir's unique process model that offers a world-class way to go parallel without fear. Finally, use the most common libraries like Ecto, Phoenix, and Oban to build a real-world SMS application. Now's the time. Dive in and learn Elixir.

Stephen Bussey
(222 pages) ISBN: 9798888650318. $48.95
*https://pragprog.com/book/sbelixir*

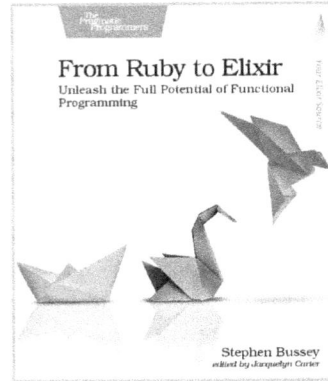

# Real-Time Phoenix

Give users the real-time experience they expect, by using Elixir and Phoenix Channels to build applications that instantly react to changes and reflect the application's true state. Learn how Elixir and Phoenix make it easy and enjoyable to create real-time applications that scale to a large number of users. Apply system design and development best practices to create applications that are easy to maintain. Gain confidence by learning how to break your applications before your users do. Deploy applications with minimized resource use and maximized performance.

Stephen Bussey
(326 pages) ISBN: 9781680507195. $45.95
*https://pragprog.com/book/sbsockets*

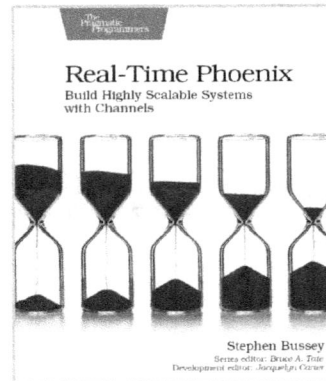

# Network Programming in Elixir and Erlang

TCP, UDP, DNS, HTTP, and more: these are the network protocols that make up the fabric of the Internet. Erlang and Elixir are the perfect fit for building network-intensive applications—the BEAM's actor model perfectly mirrors the way nodes operate in a network. Learn about networking and the power of the BEAM to write performant and reliable network applications. Create systems that are scalable, resilient, and efficient, thanks to language primitives and OTP. Take advantage of an ecosystem that has been solving network problems for more than thirty years. Learn about design patterns and common pitfalls for network applications on the BEAM.

Andrea Leopardi
(272 pages) ISBN: 9798888651056. $54.95
*https://pragprog.com/book/alnpee*

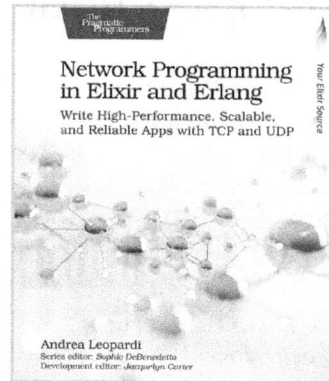

# Ash Framework

Ash Framework is the game-changing toolkit for Elixir developers. With modular, plug-and-play building blocks, Ash slashes development time, effort, and complexity, letting you do more with less code. Design declarative, customizable domain models that are easy to maintain and optimized for performance. Shift your focus to what to build, instead of how, using Ash's intuitive design principles. Tackle bigger challenges and build scalable, future-proof web applications with confidence. Elevate your Elixir skills and revolutionize your workflow with Ash.

Rebecca Le and Zach Daniel
(294 pages) ISBN: 9798888651520. $53.95
*https://pragprog.com/book/ldash*

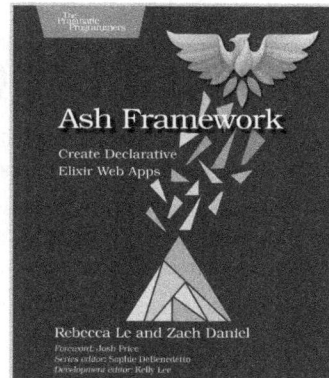

# The Pragmatic Bookshelf

The Pragmatic Bookshelf features books written by professional developers for professional developers. The titles continue the well-known Pragmatic Programmer style and continue to garner awards and rave reviews. As development gets more and more difficult, the Pragmatic Programmers will be there with more titles and products to help you stay on top of your game.

# Visit Us Online

### This Book's Home Page
*https://pragprog.com/book/jkelixir*
Source code from this book, errata, and other resources. Come give us feedback, too!

### Keep Up-to-Date
*https://pragprog.com*
Join our announcement mailing list (low volume) or follow us on Twitter @pragprog for new titles, sales, coupons, hot tips, and more.

### New and Noteworthy
*https://pragprog.com/news*
Check out the latest Pragmatic developments, new titles, and other offerings.

# Save on the ebook

Save on the ebook versions of this title. Owning the paper version of this book entitles you to purchase the electronic versions at a terrific discount.

PDFs are great for carrying around on your laptop—they are hyperlinked, have color, and are fully searchable. Most titles are also available for the iPhone and iPod touch, Amazon Kindle, and other popular e-book readers.

Send a copy of your receipt to support@pragprog.com and we'll provide you with a discount coupon.

# Contact Us

| | |
|---|---|
| Online Orders: | *https://pragprog.com/catalog* |
| Customer Service: | *support@pragprog.com* |
| International Rights: | *translations@pragprog.com* |
| Academic Use: | *academic@pragprog.com* |
| Write for Us: | *http://write-for-us.pragprog.com* |

www.ingramcontent.com/pod-product-compliance
Lightning Source LLC
Chambersburg PA
CBHW081809200326

41597CB00023B/4201